The Journal of Andrew Fuller Studies

Published in the United States of America
by The Andrew Fuller Center for Baptist Studies
The Southern Baptist Theological Seminary
2825 Lexington Road
Louisville, Kentucky 40280

© The Andrew Fuller Center for Baptist Studies 2023

All rights reserved. No part of this publication may be reproduced, stored in a retrieval system, or transmitted, in any form or by any means, without the prior permission in writing of The Andrew Fuller Center for Baptist Studies, or as expressly permitted by law, by license, or under terms agreed with the appropriate reproduction rights organization.

ISBN 978-1-77484-127-3

Printed by H&E Publishing, West Lorne, Ontario, Canada

The Journal of Andrew Fuller Studies

The Journal of Andrew Fuller Studies is an open access, double-blind peer-reviewed, scholarly journal published online biannually in February and September by the Andrew Fuller Center for Baptist Studies (under the auspices of The Southern Baptist Theological Seminary). The publication language of the journal is English. Articles that deal with the life, ministry, and thought of the Baptist pastor-theologian Andrew Fuller are very welcome, as well as essays on his friends, his Particular Baptist community in the long eighteenth century (1680s–1830s), and the global impact of his thought, known as "Fullerism."

Articles and book reviews are to follow generally the style of Kate L. Turabian, *A Manual for Writers of Research Papers, Theses, and Dissertations*, 9th ed. (Chicago, IL: University of Chicago Press, 2018). They may be submitted in British, American, Australian, New Zealand, or Canadian English. Articles should be between 5,000 and 8,000 words, excluding footnotes. Articles are to be sent to the Editor and book reviews to the Book Review Editor.

Editor:
Michael A G Haykin, ThD, FRHistS
Professor of Church History
& Director, The Andrew Fuller Center for Baptist Studies
The Southern Baptist Theological Seminary, Louisville, Kentucky
mhaykin@sbts.edu

Associate editor:
Baiyu Andrew Song, PhD, FRAS
Adjunct Course Professor
Carey Theological College
Vancouver, BC
basong@carey-edu.ca

Design editor & Book review editor:
Caleb Anthony Neel, PhD cand.
The Southern Baptist Theological Seminary, Louisville, Kentucky
cneel@sbts.edu

Editorial board:
Cindy Aalders, DPhil
Director of the John Richard Allison Library
& Assistant Professor of the History of Christianity
Regent College, Vancouver

Dustin B. Bruce, PhD
Dean & Assistant Professor of Christian Theology and Church History
Boyce College
Louisville, Kentucky

Chris W. Crocker, PhD
Pastor, Markdale Baptist Church, ON
& Associate Professor of Church History
Toronto Baptist Seminary
Toronto, Ontario

Chris Chun, PhD
Professor of Church History & Director of the Jonathan Edwards Center
Gateway Seminary
Ontario, California

Jenny-Lyn de Klerk, PhD
Editor, Book Division
Crossway
Wheaton, Illinois

Jason G. Duesing, PhD
Provost & Professor of Historical Theology
Midwestern Baptist Theological Seminary
Kansas City, Missouri

Nathan A. Finn, PhD
Provost & Dean of the University Faculty
North Greenville University
Tigerville, South Carolina

C. Ryan Griffith, PhD
Pastor, Cities Church
St. Paul, Minnesota

Peter J. Morden, PhD
Principal
Bristol Baptist College
Clifton Down
Bristol, England

Adriaan C. Neele, PhD
Director, Doctoral Program & Professor of Historical Theology
Puritan Reformed Theological Seminary
Grand Rapids, Michigan
& Research Scholar
Yale University, Jonathan Edwards Center
New Haven, Connecticut

Robert Strivens, PhD
Pastor, Bradford on Avon Baptist Church (UK)
& Lecturer in Church History
London Seminary
London, England

Tom Nettles, PhD
Senior Professor of Historical Theology
The Southern Baptist Theological Seminary
Louisville, Kentucky

Blair Waddell, PhD
Pastor, Providence Baptist Church
Huntsville, Alabama

Contents

The Journal of Andrew Fuller Studies
No. 7, September 2023

Editorial Michael A.G. Haykin	9
Articles Anglican presbyters who became Baptist pastors in the seventeenth century *Andrew Messmer*	11
The eschatology of the Calvinistic Baptist John Gill (1697–1771) examined and compared *Barry H. Howson*	23
The laying aside of "empty hands": John Gill and his theology of ordination *Alex Arrell*	45
"Nursing fathers and … nursing mothers to the Israel of God": Benjamin Beddome on praying for godly rulers *Michael A.G. Haykin*	65
William Carey (1761–1834) and his books *Austin Walker*	69
Texts & documents Thomas Williams' letter *ed. Michael A.G. Haykin*	84
"We want love": College Lane church's letter to the Northamptonshire Association *ed. Garrett M. Walden*	86
"I had far rather take one convert from Satan, than a thousand from a brother": James Hinton on Protestant catholicity *ed. Chance Faulkner*	90
Book reviews	93

Editorial

Michael A.G. Haykin

Michael A.G. Haykin is Professor of Church History and Director, The Andrew Fuller Center for Baptist Studies at The Southern Baptist Theological Seminary, Louisville, KY.

In this seventh issue of *The Journal of Andrew Fuller Studies* we have a range of articles: a determination of the university background of Baptists ministers in the seventeenth century; a couple of essays on that doyen of Baptist life in the mid-eighteenth century, John Gill; a short study on Benjamin Beddome, who left a fabulous selection of sermons that are a treasure-trove for the study of eighteenth-century Particular Baptist preaching; and an essay on William Carey's reading.

Andrew Messmer's "Anglican presbyters who became Baptist pastors in the seventeenth century" is an in-depth determination of how many of the Baptist pastors in the seventeenth university had been to university. It is a helpful correction to the idea that most of the Baptist ministers of that era were autodidacts. Despite the number of articles written on Gill in the last fifty year, studies of this remarkable pastor-theologian are still in their infancy. Barry Howson's essay on Gill's eschatology and Alex Arrell's article on his view of ordination (an anticipation of the views of the Victorian Baptist C.H. Spurgeon) are therefore most welcome. They provide two key windows on the thought of this influential Baptist author.

Our final two essays are a short study, by the editor of this journal, on Benjamin Beddome's political theology—which has become a subject of particular fascination at this point in time—and an essay on the reading of William Carey by Austin Walker. This essay originated as the 2011 annual lecture for The Evangelical Library in London. Walker has just finished a monograph on the early nineteenth-century Baptist preacher Robert Hall, Jr., which is to be published by H&E Publishing.

Profitable reading!

The Journal of Andrew Fuller Studies
7 | September 2023

Anglican presbyters who became Baptist pastors in the seventeenth century[1]

Andrew Messmer

Andrew Messmer (PhD, Evangelische Theologische Faculteit) is the academic dean of Seville Theological Seminary, Spain, associate professor at Facultad Internacional de Teología IBSTE in Spain, affiliated researcher at Evangelische Theologische Faculteit (Belgium), and editor of the *Revista Evangélica de Teología* (WEA). He lives in Santiponce, Spain, with his wife and five children, where his research interests focus on the Spanish Protestant Reformation.

Introduction

The beginning of the Baptist movement owes a great debt to the universities of Oxford and Cambridge, and the Church of England, as many early Baptists were graduates, members, and ministers of these institutions. Previous attempts to discuss the phenomenon of Anglican presbyters becoming Baptist pastors in the seventeenth century are either insufficient, due to citing limited examples, or unreliable, as they confuse rumor with demonstrable fact.[2] Thus, this article provides, for the first time, a reliable list of Anglican presbyters who became Baptist pastors during the mid to late seventeenth century, without claiming to be exhaustive, as not every instance of this phenomenon was documented and survived.[3] In addition to my

---

[1] Editor: Notice the clerical titles of "presbyter" and "priest" are used synonymously, as both words derived from the Greek word πρεσβύτερος. In Anglican documents, the term "priest" is frequently used, as "priest" is below "bishop" and above "deacon" in the three basic Anglican orders.

[2] Earlier published works provide names and stories of supposed Anglican converts to the Baptist tradition, but it is impossible or otherwise very difficult to separate fact from hearsay. For example, Thomas Crosby, *The History of the English Baptists, from the Reformation to the Beginning of the Reign of George I* (London, 1760), 3:1–162; W.T. Whitley, "Baptists and Bartholomew's Day," *Transactions of the Baptist Historical Society* 1 (1908–1909): 24–37. Possible figures that have been excluded from this study were due to insufficient information on John Miles, Samuel French, Laurence Wise, and William Woodward.

[3] This period corresponds to the founding of the Baptist movement in England. Examples of Anglican presbyters who became Baptist ministers after this time would be Baptist Wriothesley Noel (1799–1873) and Joseph Charles Philpot (1802–1869).

research, several contemporary Baptist historians have assisted in the compilation process.[4] The entries have been corroborated by the *Oxford Dictionary of National Biography* (*ODNB*), and any supplements to, or deviations from, the ODNB are based on academic works dedicated to the individuals in question.[5] The names appear in chronological order, and both General and Particular Baptists have been included, with the former being indicated with an asterisk (*) before the entry's name.[6]

List of Anglican presbyters who became Baptist pastors in the seventeenth century
1. *John Smyth (d. 1612): Smyth was a Cambridge graduate (MA, 1593), and was ordained by William Wickham (1539–1595), bishop of Lincoln, sometime between 1584 and 1595. After various appointments and preaching posts, Smyth broke with the Church of England in about February of 1607. Around January of 1609 Smyth rebaptized himself and his followers in Amsterdam, thereby starting the first Baptist church.

2. William Wroth (1575/6–c.1638/1641): an Oxford graduate (BA, 1596; MA, 1605) and an Anglican priest. By the 1610s, he held the livings of Llanfaches, Bristol, and Llanfihangel Rogiet. Perhaps as early as 1620, but certainly by 1635, he underwent a change of mind which caused him to be brought before the Court of High Commission, and in 1638 he left his living. In 1639, Henry Jessey (see no. 6) was sent by his London congregation to assist Wroth, Walter Cradock, and Henry Walter in their endeavor to reform the nucleus of the Llanfaches congregation. The church was theologically broad, but four factors strongly imply that it was broadly Baptist: (1) Henry Jessey, an important early Baptist figure, was asked for help at its founding; (2) when political factors forced the Llanfaches (and Broadmead) church to emigrate to London in 1643, some joined the congregation of Henry Jessey and others that of William Kiffin (1616–1701); (3) when the congregation returned from London to Bristol in 1645, the congregation became officially Baptist; and (4) in 1651, the church called Thomas Ewins (fl. 1651–1670) to be their pastor, who formerly had been a member of Jessey's church.[7]

3. Benjamin Cox (1595–c.1663): an Oxford graduate (BA, 1613; MA, 1617) and an Anglican priest. By 1618, he was a lecturer at All-Hallows-the-Great in London, and throughout the 1620s a preacher in several different churches, including Sampford Peverill, where in 1627 he accepted a perpetual curacy and served

---

[4] I would like to thank Michael A.G. Haykin, Larry Kreitzer, Doug Weaver, and Samuel Renihan for their kind help.

[5] I have also referenced the Clergy of the Church of England Database, https://theclergydatabase.org.uk/jsp/search/index.jsp.

[6] I have excluded the Seventh-day Baptists, such as Francis Bampfield.

[7] See Roger Hayden, "Broadmead, Bristol in the Seventeenth Century," *Baptist Quarterly* 23.8 (1970): 350–351.

until 1639 or 1640. In the winter of 1642–1643, Cox arrived in London where he joined the General Baptist congregation at Bell Alley, and in 1645 joined one of the seven Particular Baptist churches in London. In 1646, Cox signed the First London Confession (1644) on behalf of a church led by himself and its probable founder, Thomas Kilcop, and was also the author of *An Appendix to a Confession of Faith*. During c.1648–1649, Cox spent time in Bedford, where he was possibly associated with Edward Harrison (see no. 22). In 1658, Cox was instrumental in the establishment of an association of Baptist churches in the Kensworth, Bedfordshire, and Hertfordshire.

4. *Edward Barber (c.1595–1663): Barber was an Anglican clergyman who in 1637 was excommunicated from St Benet Fink, London, and identified as a Baptist.[8] His 1641 tract *A Small Treatise of Baptisme or Dipping* is notable, being the first work in England during the seventeenth century that argued for immersion as the proper mode of baptism. Along with Thomas Lamb (or Lambe, d. 1672) and others, he pastored the Bell Alley congregation in London, the most important church in the fellowship. He was instrumental in bringing General Baptist churches into association in 1645.

5. Hanserd Knollys (1598–1691): a Cambridge graduate (BA, 1627/1629) and an Anglican priest, who was ordained in 1629 by Thomas Dove (1555–1630), the bishop of Peterborough, after which Knollys was given a small living at Humberstone, Lincolnshire.[9] However, in part thanks to Puritan influence, in 1636 (or shortly thereafter) Knollys renounced his Anglican living and ordination. In 1644, Knollys became a member of Henry Jessey's congregation in London and was baptized by Jessey in June 1645. In 1645, Knollys started the church at Swan Alley (Coleman Street) in London, which was one of the first Particular Baptist congregations and apparently closed in 1678.[10] In 1646, along with Benjamin Cox (see no. 3), he subscribed to the First London Confession (1646). Although not relinquishing leadership of the Baptist church in London, in 1658 he returned to his home village in Scartho, Lincolnshire, where he was installed as vicar of St Giles, where his father and son also served.[11] Knollys was a central figure in the consolidation of the Baptist movement in England, and, in addition to being one of the seven authors who called for Baptist churches to meet in September

---

[8] The *ODNB* entry on Barber has been supplemented by Stephen Wright, "Edward Barber (c.1595–1663) and His Friends (Part 1)," *Baptist Quarterly* 41.6 (2014): 355–370.

[9] In addition to the *ODNB* entry, see Barry Howson, *Erroneous and Schismatical Opinions: The Question of Orthodoxy Regarding the Theology of Hanserd Knollys (c.1599–1691)* (Leiden: Brill, 2001).

[10] See W.T. Whitley, "Baptist Churches till 1660," *Transactions of the Baptist Historical Society* 2 (1911): 246.

[11] Kenneth C.G. Newport commented: "Quite how unusual this arrangement was in the late 1640s is not entirely clear; however, we do know that some nineteen Particular Baptists were ejected from other livings during the period from 1660 to 1662" (Newport, "Knollys, Hanserd," *ODNB*, accessed September 2, 2023, https://doi.org/10.1093/ref:odnb/15736).

1689, his name appears first among the signers of the Second London Confession (1677/1688).

6. Henry Jessey (1601–1663): a Cambridge graduate (BA, 1623; MA, 1626) and an Anglican priest in the diocese of Llandaff in 1626.[12] Shortly thereafter he was transferred to London. However, in June of 1645, he was baptized by Hanserd Knollys (see no. 5), and appears to have continued as pastor, although he refused to impose rebaptism as a condition of communion.[13] By 1650, Jessey was a Sunday afternoon preacher in the Particular Baptist church at Swan Alley, and a weekday lecturer at All-Hallows-the-Great on Thames Street in London.

7. John Tombes (1602–1676): an Oxford graduate (BA, 1621; MA, 1624; BD, 1631) and an Anglican priest, who was ordained in the late 1620s.[14] He served in various capacities such as preacher at Worcester, vicar of Leominster, Herefordshire, lecturer at All Saints, Bristol, and rector of St Gabriel Fenchurch, London. His doubts regarding the scriptural basis for infant baptism began in c.1627, and by 1644 he was fully persuaded by the case against infant baptism. Upon returning to Bewdley as curate of the town's chapel in 1646, he founded a small Baptist congregation, and trained some of members for the Baptist ministry. Upon leaving Bewdley in 1650, he continued to foster Baptist congregations elsewhere. Tombes never left the Church of England but was ejected in 1662 under the *Act of Uniformity*.[15]

8. *Samuel Fisher (1604–1665): an Oxford graduate (BA, 1627; MA, 1630) and an Anglican priest. By 1645 he was appointed vicar of All Saints', the parish church of Lydd, but sometime before 1649 he resigned and joined the Baptist congregation. In 1654 he was one of the thirteen "Messengers" sent to the national assembly of General Baptist churches. In 1655 or 1656, Fisher became a Quaker, thus ending his seven or eight-year Baptist ministry.[16]

9. *Henry Denne (1605/6?–1666): a Cambridge graduate (BA, 1625; MA, 1628) and was ordained at St David's in 1630. He served as curate at Pirton, Hertfordshire, for about ten years. By 1643 he adopted Baptist views and began attending the

---

[12] Alsoe see Jason Duesing, *Henry Jessey: Puritan Chaplain, Independent and Baptist Pastor, Millenarian Politician and Prophet* (Mountain Home, AR: BorderStone Press, 2016).

[13] The church, which then was more Separatist than strictly Baptist, was founded in 1616 by Henry Jacob, after his return from the Netherlands in that same year. Jacob was succeeded by John Lothropp and then by Jessey. This congregation was influential for the formation and development of the Baptist churches in England.

[14] Also see Mike Renihan, *Antipaedobaptism in the Thought of John Tombes: An Untold Story from Puritan England* (Auburn, MA: B&R, 2001).

[15] Although he never became a Baptist, Thomas Barlow (1608/9–1691), bishop of Lincoln, confessed his doubts over paedobaptism to John Tombes.

[16] His most remarkable work during his Baptist period was *Baby-Baptism Meer Babism* (1653) which was republished under the title *Christianismus redivivus, Christ'ndom both Unchrist'ned and New-Christ'ned* (1655, 1669).

Bell Alley Baptist Church in London.[17] He was then sent out as an evangelist to Bedfordshire, Cambridgeshire, and Huntingdonshire, where he established congregations at Fenstanton and Warboys.[18] In 1645 he preached in London, Rochester, Chatham, and Canterbury. By 1653 he was active in Fenstanton and in 1654 was sent to Canterbury to minister. He then moved and died in Rochester.

10. Roger Williams (c.1606–1683): a Cambridge graduate (BA, 1627) and an Anglican priest. In 1639, he established the first Baptist church in the English colony of Providence but left the church four months later, praying only with his wife for the rest of his life.

11. Christopher Blackwood (1607/8–1670): a Cambridge graduate (BA, 1625; MA, c. 1628) and was ordained a priest in the diocese of London on June 08, 1628.[19] He then served as vicar of Stockbury, Kent, in 1631, curate of Rye, Sussex, from 1632 to 1635, minister at Scituate in Plymouth Colony, New England in 1640, and rector of Staplehurst, Kent, from 1642 to 1644. However, in 1644 he resigned after embracing Baptist tenets upon hearing the General Baptist Francis Cornwell (see no. 12) preached at Cranbrook, Kent. He was baptized by William Jeffery (1616–1693), the General Baptist messenger (or superintendent). Between 1653 and 1670, he pastored several Particular Baptist churches in Ireland, such as Wexford and Dublin, and London.

12. Francis Cornwell (fl. mid-17th century): Little is known about Cornwell other than that he was the vicar of Marden, Kent, and that he became Baptist in about 1649 and continued his new ministry in Marden where he pastored a Particular Baptist church.[20]

13. William Britten (fl. mid-17th century): Little is known about Britten other than that he was an ordained clergyman in the Anglican church, and he left sometime after 1649 for the Baptist congregation, and in 1654 he published *The Moderate Baptist*.[21]

14. John Wigan (d. 1665): a Cambridge graduate (BA, 1633/4) and an Anglican

---

[17] Denne would have coincided with Benjamin Cox at the Bell Alley church sometime during c.1643–1645. Cox, however, then became a Particular Baptist.

[18] William Dell, previously rector of Yielden and master of Gonville and Caius College, Cambridge, was also present in Bedfordshire after his resignation and ejection in 1660. He may have had some contact with, or influence on, Baptist persons and churches in the Bedfordshire area before his death in 1669 (e.g., John Bunyan), but his main influence seem to have been on the Quakers.

[19] Also see Malcolm B. Yarnell, III, "Christopher Blackwood, 1605–1670," in *The British Particular Baptists*, ed. Michael A.G. Haykin and Terry Wolever, rev. ed. (Springfield, MO: Particular Baptist Press, 2019), 1:117–149.

[20] There is no entry for Francis Cornwell in the ODNB. The following information comes from W.T. Whiteley, "Sandhurst Bicentenary," *Baptist Quarterly* 5.7 (1931): 323.

[21] There is no entry for William Britten in the ODNB. The following information comes from H. Adis, "Baptist Literature till 1688," *Transactions of the Baptist Historical Society* 1.2 (1909): 120.

priest. In 1642 he was appointed curate of Gorton, Lancashire, and shortly thereafter was moved to be preacher at St Barnabas' Church, Heapey, where he stayed until 1644.[22] In 1644 he was named curate of Birch Chapel (Anglican), where he introduced congregational principles and later resigned in 1651 or 1652. About 1648 he became a Baptist, and in 1649 or 1650 he gathered a Baptist congregation in Manchester. By 1654, the Baptist congregation acquired space for worship, and it is possible that he was one of the few Baptist ministers who received an allowance from the state. He appears to have left Manchester for London sometime in the late 1650s.

15. Christopher Feake (1611/2–1682/3): a Cambridge graduate (BA, 1632; MA, 1635) and Anglican clergyman. From 1637 to 1654, he was the vicar of several parishes, the last of which was located at All-Hallows-the-Great, London. By 1651, he was involved in the Particular Baptist church meeting in All-Hallows-the-Great and, with John Simpson (see no. 17), was a founding figure in the Fifth Monarchy movement. In about 1657, he was opposed by Simpson, Henry Jessey, and William Kiffin for his renewed verbal attack on the government.

16. Daniel Dyke (1614–1688): a Cambridge graduate (MA, 1636) and an Anglican priest ordained in about 1636. He was appointed vicar of Eastwick, Hertfordshire. In 1645 he was briefly appointed rector of St Matthew's, London, and in 1650 was appointed rector of Much Hadham, Hertfordshire. Around this time, he embraced General Baptist principles and in 1660 resigned his living. In 1668, following a year of probationary preaching, Dyke was appointed a joint elder with William Kiffin for the Bishopsgate Particular Baptist congregation in London (later Devonshire Square), where he served until his death in 1688.

17. John Simpson (1614/5–1662): an Oxford graduate (BA, 1635; MA, 1638). He held lectureships at St Dunstan's and St Botolph's in London. In 1647 he became pastor of the Particular Baptist church meeting at All-Hallows-the-Great, London. In 1651/2, with the help and support of Christopher Feake, the Fifth Monarchy movement was born in this church. In 1659, he was briefly reinstalled as rector of Bishopsgate, but he was removed in 1660. Although a credobaptist himself, he never made it a requisite at his church.

18. William Kaye (1615–1690): a Cambridge graduate (BA, 1636/7) and an Anglican priest.[23] By 1640 he was curate of Stokesley in North Yorkshire. By 1650 he rejected the authority of bishops and was pastor to a church with Baptist leanings in Stokesley. In 1653, Kaye and nineteen of his church members were baptized by,

---

[22] There is no entry for John Wigan in the ODNB. The following information comes from T. Dowley, "John Wigan and the First Baptists of Manchester," *Baptist Quarterly* 25.4 (1973): 151–164.

[23] There is no entry for William Kaye in the ODNB. The following information comes from Stephen Copson, "Advocate of the Reformed Protestant Religion: The Writings (1645–58) of William Kaye, Yorkshire Puritan," *Baptist Quarterly* 35.6 (1994): 279–293.

or with the support of, Thomas Tillam (d. c.1674).[24]

19. Anthony Palmer (1616–1679): an Oxford graduate (BA, 1638; MA, 1641) and an ordained minister. By 1660, he moved to London where he led a mixed Baptist–Congregationalist congregation at Pinners' Hall with George Fownes (see below) and was one of five main preachers at All-Hallows-the-Great in late 1661. He was licensed as a Congregationalist in 1672.

20. George Fownes (fl. mid-17th century): the vicar of High Wycombe and by 1662 he became co-minister with Anthony Palmer (see no. 19) of the mixed Baptist–Congregationalist congregation at Pinners' Hall.[25] After Palmer's death, Fownes succeeded Thomas Hardcastle (see no. 28) as the pastor of the Broadmead congregation in Bristol.

21. Vavasor Powell (1617–1670): probably an Oxford graduate. Though the ODNB states that he "was never ordained in any of the orders of the Church of England, but probably worked as a schoolmaster in Clun," the record of his own testimony relates his preaching at the Establishment in Clun before 1640, where he officiated as curate.[26] Although he was never baptized as a believer, he led his church toward Baptist principles, which accepted both paedo- and credobaptism as valid terms of communion. According to W.T. Whitley (1861–1947), Powell was present, probably as a pastor, at All-Hallows-the-Great in London.[27]

22. Edward Harrison (c.1618–1673/1689): a graduate of Cambridge (BA, 1637/8) and Oxford (1640) and vicar of Kensworth, Bedfordshire.[28] About 1645 Harrison adopted Baptist views and resigned his vicarage, although by 1642 he was already in some way associated with Baptists such as Mark Lucar (d. 1676), Thomas Kilcop, Benjamin Cox, and Richard Graves. By 1650, he appears to be involved in leading the Baptist church of Kensworth, and in 1651 he signed the third edition of the First London Confession (1644). From 1657 onward, he was active in London, specifically the Petty France church. He took part in ordaining Thomas Patient (d. 1666) and Daniel Dyke (see no. 16) as co-pastors with William Kiffin at Bishopsgate, Devonshire Square, London.[29] He was present at the Petty France church when the Second London Confession was drawn up and published.

---

[24] Tillam had been sent out by Hanserd Knollys' church at Swan Alley, Coleman Street, London.

[25] There is no entry for George Fownes in the ODNB. The following information comes from "The Hollis Family and Pinners' Hall," *Baptist Quarterly* 1.2 (1922): 78–81.

[26] See *Life of the Rev. Vavasor Powell* (London: Religious Tract Society, 1799), 11.

[27] See Whitley, "Baptist Churches till 1660," 246.

[28] There is no entry for Edward Harrison in the ODNB. The following information comes from W.T. Whitley, "Edward Harrison of Petty France," *Baptist Quarterly* 7.5 (1935): 214–220; Jeremy Walker, "Edward Harrison ca.1618–ca.1673," in *British Particular Baptists*, 1:171–193. Samuel Renihan has indicated in a personal communication that Edward Harrison was born in 1619 and died in 1673 (Correspondence with Samuel Renihan, November 26, 2022).

[29] William Kiffin was the pastor of the Bishopsgate church from about 1644 until his death in 1701.

23. *Lawrence Wise (c. 1621–1692): Wise remains a shadowy figure but was an Anglican presbyter who later became a General Baptist pastor.[30] He ministered in Goodman's Fields, London.

24. John Pendarves (1622/3–1656): an Oxford graduate (BA, 1642) and vicar of St Helen's church in Abingdon, Berkshire, probably from 1644 to 1649, as his date of ordination is unknown.[31] Pendarves embraced Baptist beliefs in the later 1640s. In 1650, or shortly after, he took on the formal leadership of the Particular Baptist congregation in Abingdon. Together with Benjamin Cox (see no. 3), the Abingdon Association was established in 1652 to coordinate upwards of twelve Baptist churches in the region.

25. *John Gosnold (1626?–1678): matriculated to Cambridge in 1646 but left without graduation. He was later ordained as a presbyter in the Anglican Church and served as the chaplain to Thomas Grey, Lord Grey of Groby (c.1623–1657). Although Gosnold was approved by the Westminster Assembly in 1650, he became a General Baptist by 1654 and founded a congregation in Paul's Alley at Barbican, London. It became the wealthiest Baptist church in London and maintained a library for ministers. Along with Hanserd Knollys (see no. 5), William Kiffin, Daniel Dyke (see no. 16), Thomas Delaune (d. 1685), and Henry Forty (d. 1692/3), Gosnold published *The Baptists Answer to Mr Obed. Wills* (1675). It appears that the Paul's Alley congregation dissolved in 1768.[32]

26. Charles Marie de Veil (1630–1685/1691): son of Rabbi David Vail de Weil, who presided over the synagogue in Metz, Germany (later France).[33] In 1654 de Veil became a Roman Catholic and was subsequently ordained as a priest of the Augustinian order at Angers. Due to the increasing influence of Jansenism and de Weil defended its theses in his 1674 doctoral defense. De Veil was received into the Anglican Church in 1678 and was soon allowed into the ministry.[34] In 1684, he became a Baptist and became friendly with Nehemiah Coxe (d. 1689) at the Petty France church, London. He became a Baptist minister and was one of the few who received remuneration for his service, which he did until his death. During the last years of his life, he pastored the Baptist church in Gracechurch Street, London.

---

[30] There is no entry for Lawrence Wise in the ODNB. The following information comes from a personal email I received from Samuel Renihan, and Adam Taylor, *The English General Baptists of the Seventeenth Century* (London: T. Bore, 1818), 1:246–247.

[31] Also see Larry Kreitzer, "The Fifth Monarchist John Pendarves: Chaplain to Colonel Thomas Rainborowe's Regiment of Foot (1645–7)," *Baptist Quarterly* 43.2 (2009): 112–122.

[32] See Whitley, "Baptist Churches till 1660," 247.

[33] Samuel Renihan indicated that de Veil died in 1686 (Correspondence with Samuel Renihan, November 26, 2022).

[34] Interestingly, Henry Compton (c.1632–1713), bishop of London, did not insist on de Veil's re-ordination; instead, he took the oath of supremacy and promise conformity to the Book of Common Prayer and the Thirty-Nine Articles.

27. Edmund Hickeringill (1631–1708): a Cambridge graduate (BA, 1651; MA, 1652) and an Anglican priest. In 1652 Hickeringill was baptized and became a member of Thomas Tillam's Baptist church in Hexham, Northumberland, where Hickeringill became a minister later that year.[35] In 1653 he was excommunicated for being a "desperate atheist."

28. Thomas Hardcastle (1637–1678): a Cambridge graduate (BA, 1656) and vicar of Bramham, near Leeds. In 1674, after a three-year trial, Hardcastle was appointed as minister of Broadmead Baptist Church, Bristol.[36] Although a convinced Baptist, and one who argued for full immersion, he did not make believer's baptism a term of communion.[37]

29. Richard Adams (d. after 1709): Adams was an Anglican clergyman who studied under John Tombes in Worchestershire and served as vicar at Humberstone (near Leicester) until 1661.[38] After the Great Ejection in 1662, Adams first ministered the General Baptist church at Shad Thames, London, and then the Particular Baptist church at Bishopsgate, Devonshire Square, London, with William Kiffin in 1690, after the death of Daniel Dyke (see no. 16). Adams was a signer of the Second London Confession.

30. Richard Claridge (1649–1723): an Oxford graduate (BA, 1670) and ordained in the King Henry VII Lady Chapel at Westminster Abbey in 1672 and ministered in Worcestershire for nearly twenty years. He became dissatisfied with Anglicanism and received credobaptism on October 21, 1691. In 1692, he was named minister at the Bagnino, a Baptist meeting house in London, where he stayed till 1696, when he became a Quaker.

Synthesis and Observations

As was stated in the introduction, the preceding list is not exhaustive, but representative, as it only contains the names of those Anglican presbyters in the seventeenth century who became Baptist ministers and whose embrace of Baptist

---

[35] Tillam did not become a Sabbatarian until c. 1656.

[36] Edward Terrill (1635–1686) was a co-minister of the Broadmead church. In 1679 he left money and property to be used in establishing a training center for Baptist ministers, which came to fruition in 1720 with the Bristol Academy.

[37] With their open communion position, two churches in London (Pinners' Hall under Anthony Palmer [1618–1678] and George Fownes; and All-Hallows-the-Great), one in Bristol (Broadmead under Thomas Hardcastle), and one in Bedford (Bedford Meeting under John Bunyan [1628–1688]) were, at least for a time, mixed congregations of both paedo- and credobaptists.

[38] There is no entry for Richard Adams (the Baptist, not the Presbyterian) in the *ODNB*. The following information comes from W.T. Whitley, "Baptists and Bartholomew' Day," *Transactions of the Baptist Historical Society* 1 (1908–1909): 35; Alan Betteridge, "Early Baptists in Leicestershire and Rutlane (IV) Particular Baptists; Later Developments," *Baptist Quarterly* 26 (1976): 210–211). Samuel Renihan believed that Adams died in 1716 (Correspondence with Samuel Renhihan, November 26, 2022).

principles have been confirmed by previous studies. How many more shared their experience remains unknown. What is the significance of this study? I would like to suggest two ways these findings can help us appreciate the Anglican–Baptist connection.

First, while a large segment of the seventeenth-century Baptist movement was led by laymen, there were also educated and experienced ministers among the Baptists leaders.[39] All but a handful of men surveyed here had Oxbridge education, and all served previously as presbyters in the Church of England. Thus, they were able to offer their knowledge of scripture, doctrine, philosophy, linguistics, and other crucial topics, to the Baptist movement as it was forming its identity in the mid to late-seventeenth century.

Second, some played a significant part in key Particular Baptist confessional statements during the seventeenth century. Benjamin Cox (no. 3), Hanserd Knollys (no. 5), and Edward Harrison (no. 22) were involved in the drafting of the First London Confession (1644/1646). Knollys, Harrison, Richard Adams (no. 29), and Daniel Dyke (no. 16) were involved in the drafting of the Second London Confession (1677/1688). It could be imagined how their training at Oxbridge and ministry in the Establishment had significantly helped them articulate their Baptist beliefs with precision, clarity, and balance.

Finally, I suggest that it is possible that Baptists can make a weak claim to "apostolic succession," although probably not as it has been traditionally understood. Since the Council of Nicaea (325), "apostolic succession" was understood to be passed down through the line of bishops—understood as a distinct office from presbyters—and only when at least three bishops perform the ordination, or express written consent. The text reads thus:

> It is by all means desirable that a bishop should be appointed by all the bishops of the province. But if this is difficult because of some pressing necessity or the length of the journey involved, let at least three come together and perform the ordination, but only after the absent bishops have taken part in the vote and given their written consent. But in each province the right of confirming the proceedings belongs to the metropolitan bishop.[40]

There is no known example of one, let alone three, Anglican bishops who became Baptist pastors, and thus some may be led to conclude that no case can be made at all for apostolic succession within the Baptist tradition. However, two arguments can be used in response. First, it must be recognized that this way of understanding

---

[39] The first General Baptist church in England began in 1612, and the first Particular Baptist church in about 1633. Their numbers rapidly increased in the subsequent decades, and by the close of the Commonwealth period (1649–1660), there were about 115 General Baptist congregations in England and about 131 Particular Baptist congregations (Whitley, "Baptist Churches till 1660," 236). Thus, it seems that only a fraction of these congregations was led by former Anglican presbyters.

[40] Norman Tanner, ed., *Decrees of the Ecumenical Councils* (London: Sheed & Ward, 1990), 1:7.

"apostolic succession" is an ecclesiastical rule, or "canon," and not a New Testament command. Thus, were one to depart from this pattern, as Baptists did in the seventeenth century, one could not be accused of disobeying scripture, but rather of deviating from agreed upon church practice. This is admittedly a significant issue, but one which could be remedied through dialogue and over time. While Anglicans and other Christian traditions may have been right to be suspicious of the new Baptist movement at its beginning, over the centuries it has proven itself to be an orthodox movement that rightly upholds the core teaching of the one, holy, catholic, and apostolic church. Second, throughout history, theologians and pastors have doubted whether there is any essential difference between presbyters and bishops. Thus, for example, Jerome (d. 420) famously wrote:

> It is therefore the very same priest, who is a bishop, and before there existed men who are slanderers by instinct, [before] factions in the religion, and [before] it was said to the people, "I am of Paul, I am of Apollos, but I am of Cephas," the churches were governed by a common council of the priests. But after each one began to think that those whom he had baptized were his own and not Christ's, it was decreed for the whole world that one of the priests should be elected to preside over the others, to whom the entire care of the church should pertain, and the seeds of schism would be removed. ... If someone thinks that this is our opinion, but not that of the Scriptures—that bishop and priest are one, and that one is the title of age, the other of this duty—let him reread the apostle's words to the Philippians when he says [NB: Jerome cites and discusses several NT texts]. These things [have been said] in order to show that to the men of old the same men who were the priests were also the bishops; but gradually, as the seed beds of dissensions were eradicated, all solicitude was conferred on one man. Therefore, just as the priests know that by the custom of the church they are subject to the one who was previously appointed over them, so the bishops know that they, more by custom than by the truth of the Lord's arrangement, are greater than the priests.[41]

Similarly, the recently published "Cyprus Statement" signed by Anglican and Orthodox communions has concluded,

> Historically it is safe to conclude that the apostles did not hand on a fixed ministerial structure to a college of bishops as part of a clearly-defined threefold order of bishops, presbyters and deacons. The picture is one of gradual development from various forms of an episcope always present, into a pattern of one bishop in each local church, who functioned at a local level without any

---

[41] Jerome, *St. Jerome's Commentaries on Galatians, Titus, and Philemon*, trans. Thomas Scheck (Notre Dame, IN: University of Notre Dame Press, 2010), 289–290.

centralised control.[42]

If these and other authorities are correct, then if one were to have three presbyters present at an ordination service, then apostolic succession would continue through to the next generation.

In light of the evidence presented here, we know that in some Baptist churches there were multiple pastors present who formerly had been Anglican presbyters: Pinners' Hall had Anthony Palmer and George Fownes; Petty France had Benjamin Cox and Edward Harrison; Swan Alley had Hanserd Knollys and Henry Jessey; Bishopsgate had Daniel Dyke and Richard Harrison (and Thomas Patient who, along with Daniel Dyke, was ordained by Edward Harrison); and All Hallows-the-Great—the controversial Fifth Monarchist site—had Henry Jessey, John Simpson, Samuel Highland, Vavasor Powell, and Christopher Feake.[43] Many of the Particular and General Baptist pastors were in fellowship with each other, and either implicitly recognized each other as ordained ministers or explicitly participated in ordaining the subsequent generation of ministers, as Edward Harrison is a good example. While it must wait for subsequent research to see if this practice has continued down to the present day, it does seem fair to assert that, if one recognizes no qualitative distinction between presbyters and bishops with respect to the ability to ordain, then apostolic succession had continued in some Baptist churches in the seventeenth century.[44]

---

[42] *The Church of the Triune God. The Cyprus Statement agreed by the International Commission for Anglican-Orthodox Theological Dialogue 2006* (London: Anglican Communion Office, 2006), 60.

[43] Regarding General Baptists, the Bell Alley was ministered by Edward Barber and Henry Denne, and was briefly attended by Benjamin Cox. The Particular Baptist in Bristol was pastored by Thomas Hardcastle and his successor, George Fownes, but they do not seem to have overlapped.

[44] By means of comparison, it seems that Baptists could make a claim similar to, although admittedly weaker than, the one Reformed and Methodist churches make to apostolic succession.

The Journal of Andrew Fuller Studies
7 | September 2023

The eschatology of the Calvinistic Baptist John Gill (1697–1771) examined and compared[1]

Barry H. Howson

Barry Howson is the Dean of Heritage College and Seminary in Cambridge, Ontario, Canada. He graduated with his PhD from McGill University, Montreal, in Church History, specializing in early British Baptist history.

One of the enduring figures of Baptist history is the eighteenth-century Calvinist John Gill whose commentaries, treatises, and systematic theology continue to be published. In the past fifty years numerous articles, books, and dissertations have been written on Gill's theology.[2] For example, in *The Life and Thought of John Gill (1697–1771): A Tercentennial Appreciation*, edited by Michael A.G. Haykin,

---

[1] I want to thank Dr. Michael A.G. Haykin for his careful reading of this essay and for offering some helpful suggestions.

[2] Robert Edward Seymour, "John Gill, Baptist Theologian (1697–1771)" (PhD diss., University of Edinburgh, 1954); Curt Daniel, "Hyper-Calvinism and John Gill" (PhD diss., University of Edinburgh, 1983); Thomas Ascol, "The Doctrine of Grace: A critical Analysis of Federalism in the Theologies of John Gill and Andrew Fuller" (PhD diss., Southwestern Baptist Theological Seminary, 1989); B.R. White, "John Gill in London, 1719–1729: A Biographical Fragment," *Baptist Quarterly* 22 (1967–1968): 72–79; Richard A. Muller, "The Spirit and the Covenant: John Gill's Critique of the *Pactum Salutis*," *Foundations* 24 (1981): 4–14; Olin C. Robison, "The Legacy of John Gill," *Baptist Quarterly* 24 (1971–1972): 111–125; Eric Williams, "John Gill (1697–1771): Some Bicentenary Thoughts, Especially on His Work on the Song of Solomon," *Evangelical Library Bulletin* 47 (1971): 2–7; Robert Oliver, "John Gill: Orthodox Dissenter," *Strict Baptist Historical Society Bulletin* 23 (1996): 3–18; Graham Harrison, *Dr. John Gill and His Teaching* (London: Evangelical Library, 1971); John R. Broome, *Dr. John Gill* (Harpenden, Hertfordshire: Gospel Standard Trust, 1991); John W. Brush, "John Gill's Doctrine of the Church," in *Baptist Concepts of the Church*, ed. Winthrop Still Hudson (Philadelphia: Judson, 1959): 53–70; George Ella, *John Gill and the Cause of God and Truth* (Eggleston, Durham: Go Publications, 1995); David Mark Rathel, "Was John Gill a Hyper-Calvinist? Determining Gill's Theological Identity," *Baptist Quarterly* 48.1 (2017): 47–59; Rathel, "John Gill and the History of Redemption as Mere Shadow: Exploring John Gill's Doctrine of the Covenant of Redemption," *Journal of Reformed Theology* 4.11 (2017): 477–400; Rathel, "A Case Study in Baptist Catholicity: The Scriptures and the Tradition in the Theology of John Gill," *Baptist Quarterly* 49.3 (2018): 1–9. A recent series of reflections on the Book of Revelation by Chip Thornton's blog, Know.Grow.Go., https://g3min.org.

Gill's doctrine of baptism, his spirituality, his view of the law, his soteriology, and his ecclesiology were examined.[3] However, as in past studies there is little discussion of Gill's eschatology in this otherwise excellent work. This, I believe, is an unfortunate omission not only for a full account of Gill's thought but also for a better understanding of eighteenth-century English evangelicalism. For these reasons alone a study of Gill's eschatology is certainly warranted. Recently, this omission has been answered with an article by Crawford Gribben, entitled, "John Gill and Puritan Eschatology."[4] Gribben has published an excellent study of Gill's eschatology in relation to seventeenth-century puritan eschatology using Gill's *Body of Divinity*.

Why, then, the need for a further examination of this subject? First, our study will be a more thorough examination of Gill's eschatology using his commentaries and treatises as well as his *Body of Divinity*. Second, we will compare Gill's eschatology with the postmillennial eschatology of Andrew Fuller (1754–1815), the most important Baptist theologian next to Gill, of the eighteenth century. Postmillennialism was present from the early part of the seventeenth century, and by Gill's day was the dominant eschatological teaching in England and America.[5] It later became one of the motivating forces behind the modern missionary movement beginning with the Particular Baptist William Carey (1761-1834).[6] Therefore, since Gill is the premier eighteenth-century Particular Baptist theologian we must examine his eschatology to see how it differs from the dominant theology in this tradition in the eighteenth century.

A third reason for a further examination of Gill's eschatology is missiological.

---

[3] Michael A.G. Haykin, ed., *The Life and Thought of John Gill (1697--771): A Tercentennial Appreciation* (Leiden: Brill, 1997).

[4] Crawford Gribben, "John Gill and Puritan Eschatology," *Evangelical Quarterly* 73.4 (2001), 311-326.

[5] The Anglican scholar Daniel Whitby (1638-1726) has been considered the father of postmillennialism. His postmillennialist thought appeared in his 1703 essay, *A Treatise of the Millennium: Shewing That It Is Not a Reign of Persons Raised from the Dead, but of the Church Flourishing Gloriously for a Thousand Years After the Conversion of the Jews, and the Flowing-In of All Nations to them Thus Converted to the Christian Faith*. This essay was appended to his widely read book *Paraphrase and Commentary on the New Testament*. Le Roy Edwin Froom in his four volume history of prophecy (*The Prophetic Faith of Our Fathers* (Washington, DC: Review and Herald Publishing Assocation, 1948], 651–655) has argued that Whitby is the father of postmillennialism. This view is somewhat perpetuated by a present-day writer on eschatology, see Stanley Grenz, *The Millennial Maze* (Downers Grove: InterVarsity Press, 1992], 68–69. There is no doubt that Whitby was a populariser of postmillennialism in the eighteenth century but he certainly was not the originator. Its origins can be traced to Thomas Brightman (1562-1607), and its development in the seventeenth century by men like the Congregationalist John Cotton (1585-1652) and the Particular Baptist Hanserd Knollys (1599–1691). Postmillennial eschatology can also be found in the works of John Owen (1616-1683) and John Howe (1630-1705), and in the Congregationalist confession, the Savoy Declaration (1658). For some of this history see Iain Murray, *The Puritan Hope* (Edinburgh: Banner of Truth, 1971); Bryan Ball, *The Great Expectation* (Leiden: Brill, 1975), 168-170; Peter Toon, "The Latter-Day Glory," in *Puritans, The Millennium & The Future of Israel*, ed. Peter Toon (Cambridge: James Clarke, 1970), 23–41; and James De Jong, *As the Waters Cover the Sea: Millennial Expectations in the Rise of Anglo-American Missions 1640-1810* (Kampen, the Netherlands: J.H. Kok, 1970).

[6] See De Jong, *As the Waters*, 177-181.

It is undoubtedly true that eschatological beliefs affect one's actions and even one's overall theology. This is obvious from studies that have been done on religion and politics in seventeenth-century England and eighteenth-century America.[7] It is also true of nineteenth and twentieth-century eschatology in modern evangelicalism.[8] One excellent example is William Carey and the Baptist Missionary Society. One important reason that the Society was founded, and that Carey went to India was his hope of the fulfilment of the latter-day glory. Andrew Fuller, John Sutcliff (1752–1814), John Ryland, Jr. (1753–1825), and Carey believed the millennium was about to dawn with the conversion of the Gentiles as promised in Romans 11. Consequently, Carey believed Christians should "concur with God" in promoting his work and ultimately fulfilling his promise of the world-wide conversion of the heathen.[9] Their eschatology was a major factor in their missionary endeavours. Did Gill's eschatology affect his actions in evangelism and missions concerning the conversion of the heathen? James De Jong believes that it did in two contradictory ways. He states that Gill's eschatology "undoubtedly contributed to [the] rebirth of missions" among Particular Baptists in the 1790s but that some of his eschatology also "fostered a complacency regarding their responsibility in influencing the course of history" and so their involvement in the missionary endeavours of the same period.[10] Is De Jong's statement true? Did Gill's eschatology affect his missiology? And if it is true, his eschatology not only affected his own thoughts and actions regarding missions, but it probably influenced many readers of his generation and the next. We know that his eschatological writings were read by many even into the nineteenth-century, and so his eschatological views through his works affected succeeding generations.[11] For example, John Ryland, Sr. (1723–1792) was one of Gill's friends whose concept of world missions and evangelism

[7] For seventeenth-century England see, for example, Tai Liu, *Discord in Zion: The Puritan Divines and the Puritan Revolution 1640–1660* (The Hague, the Netherlands: Martinus Nijoff, 1973); Bernard Capp, *The Fifth Monarchy Men: A Study in Seventeenth-century English Millenarianism* (London: Faber and Faber, 1972); Paul Christianson, *Reformers and Babylon: English Apocalyptic Visions from the Reformation to the Eve of the Civil War* (Toronto: University of Toronto Press, 1978). For the eighteenth century see, for example, the essays on the pre-revolutionary period in D.G. Hart, ed., *Reckoning with the Past* (Grand Rapids: Baker, 1995), 61–128; Ruth Block, *Visionary Millennium: Millennial Themes in American thought, 1756–1800* (New York: Cambridge University Press, 1985).

[8] For the nineteenth and twentieth centuries consider the Baptist William Miller (1782–1849) who believed Christ was going to return in 1843, and so made preparations for it. Or think of the prophetic influence on American policies and actions toward Israel.

[9] De Jong, *As the Waters*, 175–181.

[10] De Jong, *As the Waters*, 156–157, 176. Interestingly, Gribben implies that Gill did not have an anti-missionary bias when he writes, "Despite numerous accusations of an anti-missionary bias, it seems clear that Gill expected the gospel to sweep the earth" (Gribben, "John Gill and Puritan Eschatology," 317). But for Gill this "sweep of the earth" will take place only after the destruction of antichrist and the call of the Jews which Gill predicted would not occur for at least one hundred to a hundred and fifty years after his writing. Consequently, the spread of the gospel to the Gentiles around the world would have to wait that time. Is this not, at least, an anti-missionary bias for the latter half of the eighteenth century and most of the nineteenth?

[11] De Jong, *As the Waters*, 162, 164, 176. Gribben, "John Gill and Puritan Eschatology," 326.

was affected by Gillite eschatology. In September 1785 he was purported to have said to William Carey concerning the latter's suggestion of world evangelism: "Young man, sit down. When God pleases to convert the heathen, he will do it without your aid or mine."[12] This statement is often seen as resulting from his high Calvinism, but it certainly has as much to do with his eschatology as it does his soteriology. Ryland was one of the many in that day whose eschatology influenced his concept of world missions.[13] Concerning the influence of Gill's eschatology, John Rippon (1751–1836), Gill's biographer and pastoral successor, wrote in the early nineteenth century:

> [Gill's] single Sermons, on this subject [sacred prediction], have been, of late years, some of the most popular of his works; and their deserved value has caused them to pass through several editions. These *Sermons*, with the two folio volumes on the *Prophets*, and his Exposition of the *Revelation*, have gained him unfading honours, and induced such who have made those parts of the divine writings their study, to say, that if the works of Dr. Gill pre-eminently embrace almost every branch of sacred theology, *prophecy is his forte*.[14]

His influence in eschatology was so great among Baptists that during the "Second Great Awakening" they either followed Gill's or Andrew Fuller's perspective.[15] Gill's eschatology for missiological reasons therefore needs a thorough examination.

For the above reasons a further study of Gill's eschatology is certainly warranted. This article, therefore, examines Gill's eschatology by presenting a systematic overview of Gill's eschatology, and in conclusion briefly compare his eschatology with that of his fellow Calvinistic Baptist Andrew Fuller to see the differences

---

[12] This a revision of Ryland's statement by Fuller.

[13] For the historical background to this event, and discussion on the historicity of the comment by Ryland, see Michael A.G. Haykin, *One Heart and One Soul: John Sutcliff of Olney, His Friends and His Times* (Darlington, Durham: Evangelical Press, 1994), 189–197. De Jong suggests that Gill's eschatology was a reason why Carey's word concerning missions to the heathen, spoken at the Northamptonshire Association meeting, was challenged (De Jong, *As the Waters*, 157).

[14] John Rippon, *A Brief Memoir of the Life and Writings of the Late Rev. John Gill, D.D.* (Reprint, Harrisonburg, VA: Gano Books, 1992), 74.

[15] De Jong, *As the Waters*, 202. Following this last reason, a fourth is that eschatology was very important to Gill himself. Rippon tells us that when Gill visited with people "he would seldom converse on trifles; but, touch the string of prophecy—the calling of the Jews—the latter-day glory ... he was engaged at once, and out of the abundance of knowledge and grace, treasured in his heart, his mouth freely spake" (Rippon, *Brief Memoir*, 119). This is confirmed by his discussion of prophecy in the preface of his two-volume commentary on the Old Testament prophets as well as numerous sermons that were published on eschatological subjects. Some of the published sermons include, *The Doctrine of the Resurrection Stated and Defended in Two Sermons* (1731); *The Watchman's Answer to the Question, What of the Night?* (1751); *The Glory of the Church in the Latter Day* (1753); *The Glorious State of the Saints in Heaven* (1756); *The Superior Happiness of the Righteous Dead to that of Living Saints* (1763).

between their two perspectives.[16]

Systematic overview[17]

This section examines the end-time events as Gill perceived how they would unfold chronologically. These events include Christ's spiritual reign, his personal reign, the resurrection of the dead, conflagration of the world, the new heavens and new earth, the millennium, the last and general judgement, the final state of the wicked in Hell, and that of the saints in heaven. Before unfolding Gill's eschatology, it is necessary to take brief of the way he viewed history from the time of Christ's ascension to the ultimate glory in heaven. Gill believed that Christ reigns at all times over all things. After Christ's ascension and the initial age of the Church, there are two future prophetic historical epochs to be fulfilled before Christ's reign in ultimate glory.[18] The first epoch Gill calls Christ's "spiritual reign" or the "latter day glory," and the second he calls Christ's "personal reign."[19]

Spiritual reign[20]

Gill believed that the spiritual reign of Christ had not yet dawned when he wrote his *Body of Divinity*. It would, however, take place "upon the rising and ascending, of the witnesses [Rev 11] into heaven … [and] be introduced upon the blowing of the seventh trumpet."[21] This future spiritual reign will be marked by three things. First, it will be similar to the present reign of Christ but marked "with greater purity and to a greater degree of perfection; both as to doctrine and practice."[22] First of all, this

---

[16] The primary sources for our understanding of Gill's eschatology is his *Body of Divinity* (1839, Atlanta, GA: Turner Lassatter, 1957) and his commentaries. His sermons and tracts will be supplemental. Gill addresses both individual and future eschatology in his *Body of Divinity*. This article only deals with the latter.

[17] For an overview of Gill's commentary on Revelation see Barry Howson, "A Survey of John Gill's Commentary of the Book of Revelation" (unpublished paper, 2008). Gill continues the historicist and symbolic-figurative interpretation of Revelation that was espoused by the most eminent British interpreters of the seventeenth century including John Napier (1550–1617), Arthur Dent (d. 1607), Thomas Brightman (1562–1607), Thomas Goodwin (1600–1680), and Joseph Mede (1586–1639), as well as Particular Baptist Hanserd Knollys (1599–1691). For Knollys' eschatology see Barry Howson, *"Erroneous and schismatical opinions": The Question of Orthodoxy in the Theology of Hanserd Knollys (1599–1691)* (Leiden: Brill, 2001).

[18] This initial Church-age began with Christ's death, resurrection, and ascension, and the coming of the Spirit at Pentecost, and was still present in Gill's day. It would end when Christ began His "spiritual reign" (one of the two future historical epochs).

[19] Gill, *Body of Divinity*, 448.

[20] See Gribben, "John Gill and Puritan Eschatology," 317–319.

[21] John Gill, *The Glory of the Church in the Latter Day* (1752), in *Sermons and Tracts* (London: W. Hardcastle, 1814), 1:93. According to Gill this reign would begin after the "time of trouble" prophesied in Dan 12:1 that will "come upon the whole world, Rev. iii. 10. as it may concern the church and the people of God, it is the last struggle of the beast, of antichrist, at the time of his downfall and ruin, when he will make his last effort; this will be the last persecution of the saints, which will be short and sharp" (Gill, *Gill's Commentary* [Grand Rapids: Baker, 1980], 4:568–569).

[22] Gill, *Body of Divinity*, 448. Gill believes that Zech. 14:6–9 is a prophecy of this spiritual reign. He believed that a dark day would precede the spiritual reign of Christ "a sort of twilight, both with respect to the

means that the ministry of the Word would be greater, that is, there would be: more light and clearness with regard to spiritual matters; greater understanding of the gospel; great agreement among ministers who preach the Word; and one doctrine of faith preached and professed by all, in other words there would be no heretics.[23] In addition, the gospel will spread out in a greater way and be preached with greater success.[24] Second, the ordinances will be restored to their primitive purity and be observed clear of such innovations and corruptions as transubstantiation and infant baptism. Third, discipline will be carried out with greater strictness and be far more agreeable to the laws and rules of Christ. Moreover, there will be no controversies about the nature of the church, its government or its officers. The churches will be as they were in the days of the apostles.[25]

This spiritual reign will not only be greater in purity but, it will be "more large and ample than now it is," that is, it will reach all over the world. Before this happens, though, two important things must take place. The first is the destruction of the anti-Christian states as well as the Antichrist himself who is the "little horn" of Daniel, the "man of sin" of 2 Thessalonians, and the two beasts of Rev 13.[26] Following the hermeneutics of the Reformation, Gill has no hesitation in identifying the antichrist as the Pope. The anti-Christian states are thus all those places where Roman Catholic Church reigns. Their destruction is accomplished by

---

light of doctrine, and spiritual joy, comfort, and experience; which is much our case now." This is when the witnesses will be slain and "great coldness and lukewarmness will seize upon professors; great darkness of error will spread itself everywhere; great sleepiness and security will fall upon all the virgins, and there will be great distress of nations." However, it is during this time that "*light* will break forth; deliverance and salvation from Popish darkness and tyranny will be wrought; the light of the Gospel will break forth, and spread itself everywhere; the light of joy and gladness will arise to all saints, and it will be a time of great spiritual peace, prosperity, and happiness." During this time "the Gospel shall be carried from east to west, and preached all the world over, to the conversion of Jews and Gentiles." According to Gill verse nine, which states "the Lord shall be King over all the earth," refers to the spiritual reign of Christ where "upon the success of the Gospel everywhere, there will be great conversions in all places; Gospel churches will be set up and ordinances administered everywhere; the earth will be filled with the knowledge of the Lord; his kingdom will be from sea to sea, from the eastern to the western one, and his dominion will reach to the ends of the earth; Popish nations, Mahometan kingdoms, Pagan ones, and all the kings of the earth, will become Christian, and submit to the sceptre of Christ's kingdom" (Gill, *Gill's Commentary*, 4:871–872).

[23] Gill says in his commentary on Zech 14:9, "There will be one true, spiritual, uniform worship and religion; there will be no different sentiments and principles in religion; nor different practices and modes of worship; nor different sects; but all agreeing in the same faith and practice, under one Lord and King, Christ Jesus" (Gill, *Gill's Commentary*, 4:872).

[24] Gill, *Body of Divinity*, 448–449. One of the chief passages he uses is Zech 14:6–9.

[25] Gill, *Body of Divinity*, 449–450.

[26] See his extended comment on the "little horn" as the Pope in Daniel 7:8. The man of sin according to Gill is "a succession of men … the whole hierarchy of Rome, monks, friars, priests, bishops, archbishops, cardinals, and especially popes, who may well be called *the man of sin*, because notoriously sinful; not only sinners, but sin itself, a sink of sin, monsters of iniquity, spiritual wickedness in high places" (Gill, *Gill's Commentary*, 6:576). He goes on in the next verse to show that popes have considered themselves God on earth. For the rise and fall of the Pope as antichrist see Gill's comment on Dan 7:24–26. For a further detailed description of the Pope as antichrist, and of his claims and teachings see Gill's comment on Dan 11:36–39.

the preaching of the gospel and the pouring out of the seven vials of God's wrath.[27] The first five vials will be poured out by the Protestant princes as they march and physically conquer the papal countries, the western antichrist, which include Germany, France, Spain, Portugal, and Italy. These countries will then become the kingdoms of Christ.[28]

The second thing that must take place before the reign of Christ reaches over the whole world is the conversion of the Jews.[29] This follows the destruction of the antichrist because the popish religion is a great stumbling block to the Jews. Gill believed that this conversion was not a civil or national one but a spiritual one, that is they will be born again *en masse* and added to the Christian churches and yet still remain a distinct people. They will then return to their land and possess it with the help of the Protestant princes who will drive out the Muslims.[30] These princes will continue to conquer the other Islamic dominions, which constitutes the fulfilment of the pouring out of the sixth vial. Consequently, the gospel will now spread to the eastern countries such as Tartary (present day Russia), Persia, China, and the Great Mogul (present day India). Now the fulness of the Gentiles will be brought in, Gentile kings will fall before Christ, and their kingdoms will be given to the saints.[31]

This spiritual reign will not only be marked by greater purity, and reach over the whole world, but it will also be a more spiritual time than the present. Primarily this means there will be a more plentiful effusion of the Spirit. This effusion will come upon the ministers and churches as well as upon the Jews and Gentiles to bring about "many and great conversions." At this time the saints will be more spiritual. They will seek more after God and have more light in the doctrines of the gospel, their conversation, their worship. They will also enjoy more of the spiritual presence of God and Christ. In addition, the graces of the Spirit of love

---

[27] Gill commented on 2 Thess 2:8: "As [by the gospel] sinners are cut to the heart, hewn and slain, convicted and converted, so by this likewise antichrist will be consumed, and is consuming." This began at the Reformation "and [he] is sensibly wasting in his power and glory every day and will ere long come to utter destruction." He shall be destroyed with the brightness of Christ's coming either in a spiritual way, when he comes in his spiritual kingdom and glory [the latter-day], by the light of the Gospel and the illuminations of his Spirit ... or in a personal manner, when he shall come to judge the quick and the dead [Second Coming]" (Gill, *Gill's Commentary*, 6:578). The destruction of antichrist and the anti-Christian states is looked at in Gill's comment on Zech 14:12–15, Dan 7:11, and the judgment of God on them in Dan 7:9–10.

[28] Gill, *Body of Divinity*, 450–451.

[29] Gill believed that this future conversion of the Jews in the latter day is prophesied in Ezek 39:25–29 (Gill, *Gill's Commentary*, 4:436–437). A key passage in the New Testament for Gill that deals with the conversion of the Jews in Rom 11:11–29. They will be grafted into their own olive tree and their conversion will be the reviving work of God among the Gentiles churches (Gill, *Gill's Commentary*, 4:100–103).

[30] For a prophecy concerning the eastern antichrist (Muslims), his power, wealth and riches, fall and ruin see Dan 11:40–45 (Gill, *Gill's Commentary*, 4:566–568). When the Jews are preparing to return to their land the Turk will be enraged and provoked, will march with an army to Judea, and will come to his end. This is also prophesied in Ezek 38:2–12, 39:1–20.

[31] Gill, *Body of Divinity*, 451–252. See Gill's comment on Ezek 39:21.

and faith will be more in exercise and there will be an abundance of peace and joy (Isa 11:6–9).[32] It is important to note that Gill sees this effusion of the Spirit taking place simultaneously with the destruction of the antichrist.[33] Christ will now stand up as the glorious head of the church, and as a triumphant conqueror over all his enemies, and take to himself his great power, and reign, and that kingdom which rightly belongs to him.[34] Gill did not speculate as how long this latter-day glory—what he calls the "Philadelphian" church-state—would last. But he did say it would end with a "Laodicean" church-state of lukewarmness, drowsiness and carnal security.[35] He suggested that this "Laodicean" church-state would last seven prophetic months or 210 years according to Ezek 39:12.[36] Following this final church-state the personal reign of Christ would begin.

Personal reign of Christ
The personal reign of Christ begins with the personal appearance of Christ from heaven followed by the resurrection of the dead saints in Christ, the conflagration of the world, the making of the new heavens and earth, the binding of Satan, and the dwelling and reigning of Christ with His saints on the new earth. This personal appearance is the Second Coming of Christ to earth which takes place after the slaying of the fourth beast of Daniel 7.[37] According to Gill this beast is antichrist

---

[32] In *The Glory of the Church in the Latter Day*, Gill stated, "This period of time ... will be remarkable for his spiritual presence among his people; when he will *come down*, in the communications of his grace, *like rain upon the mowen* [sic] *grass, as showers water the earth*; when there will be a large and plentiful effusion of this spirit; when his people in general will be more spiritual in the temper of their souls, and in the frames of their mind; more spiritual and savoury in their discourses, and in the whole of their behaviour and conversation, and will eminently worship God in spirit and truth: not that they will arrive to a perfection of spirituality; though there will be a great deal of light and glory break out, yet there will be a mixture of darkness, obscurity, and imperfection; in which this state will differ from the personal reign of Christ in the new Jerusalem" (Gill, *Sermons and Tracts*, 1:91–92).

[33] Gill, *Body of Divinity*, 452–453.

[34] Gill commenting on Dan 12:1, see Gill, *Gill's Commentary*, 4:568-69.

[35] See Gill, *Gill's Commentary*, 5:247, where he says, "There will be a general expectation of Christ being near at hand sometime before his second coming; and because such an expectation will not be answered, or Christ will not come so soon as was hoped for, and expected, a general drowsiness, and security, and unconcernedness, especially about the coming of Christ, will fall upon the churches." In addition, he states that the last days of 2 Tim 3:1–5, "may take in the general defection and apostasy of the church of Rome, as well as those times which followed the apostles, and those which will usher in the second coming of Christ" (Gill, *Gill's Commentary*, 6:637). Concerning this Laodicean church state Gill says, "There will be little left but external gifts, and outward riches and honour, upon which great stress will be laid; and there will be great boasting and bragging of them, ... the wise as well as the foolish virgins will slumber and sleep; ... immorality and profaneness will again spread in the world" (see *Sermons and Tracts*, 1:108).

[36] Gill, *Body of Divinity*, 624.

[37] It is important to note that Gill sees several comings of Christ, which are the incarnation, his second coming, and his coming powerfully in 70 AD in the destruction of Jerusalem. According to Gill the whole discourse of Matthew 24 essentially deals with this latter coming. In this passage Gill believes that Matt 24 1–41 answer the disciples questions about the destruction of Jerusalem (Gill, *Gill's Commentary*, 5:231–242). In addition, the 70 weeks of Dan 9:24 begin with the decree to rebuild Jerusalem 483 BC (Neh 2:1, 6–8) and

and the anti-Christian states. This second coming of Christ will be a "personal" and "visible" coming with the clouds of heaven in fulfilment of such texts as Dan 7:13–14, 12:1–3, Zech 14:4–5, and Mal 4:1–3.[38] Moreover, Christ will come in great glory—that of his Father, that of his own divine and human nature, and that of his holy angels. Every eye will see Christ in his human nature. Both good and bad men will see him as he "swiftly move[s] from one end of the heaven to the other." This second coming will be "sudden," "quick," and "speedy," much as a thief in the night breaks in to steal when no one knows the time.[39] He will first come in the air of the earth where he will meet the saints raised from the dead, and the living saints will then be changed and brought to him. The new earth will be prepared, and they will all descend upon the earth. Gill speculates that at this coming Christ will descend upon the Mount of Olives and the time of restitution of all things will begin.[40]

Gill is very cautious about determining the time when this appearance would take place. As he states: "It seems impracticable and impossible, to know the time of the second coming of Christ; and therefore it must be vain and needless, if not criminal, to enquire into it."[41] However, this did not stop him from offering a suggestion and from predicting what were to be the signs of Christ's return. Concerning the time of Christ's coming Gill believed that former interpreters had confounded the personal and spiritual reigns of Christ. They had located the end of the forty-two months of the reign of antichrist, the prophesying of the witnesses, the time when Jerusalem is trodden under foot by the Gentiles, and the church's wilderness experience as taking place just prior to Christ's second coming.[42] According to Gill, all of this takes place at the commencement of the

conclude with its destruction in 70 AD (Gill, *Gill's Commentary*, 4:547–550).

[38] On Daniel 7, see Gill, *Gill's Commentary*, 4:531. Also see 1 Thess 4:16 in Gill, *Gill's Commentary*, 6:560, where he says, "He descends ... in Person, in his human nature, in soul and body; in like manner as went up to heaven will he descend from thence, so as to be visible, to be seen and heard of all: he will come down from the third heaven, whither he was carried up, into which he was received, and where he is retained, until the time of the restitution of all things, and from whence the saints expect him."

[39] See his comments on 1 Thess 5:1–11 (Gill, *Gill's Commentary*, 6:562–565). For the second coming will be "sudden, and at unawares." The righteous, however, being "enlightened by the Spirit of God ... [are] not ignorant of these things, nor liable to be surprised unawares hereby" (Gill, *Gill's Commentary*, 6:562).

[40] Gill, *Body of Divinity*, 616–622. See his comment on Zech 14:4 where he says, "It seems very probable that he will descend upon that very spot of ground from whence he ascended" (Gill, *Gill's Commentary*, 4:870).

[41] Gill says in his comment on 1 Thess 5:1, "[For Paul] to write to them about the time of these things would be trifling and unnecessary; would be an idle speculation, and indulging a vain curiosity; and, besides, was impracticable: for that day and hour knows no man: the times and seasons the Father hath put in his own power" (Gill, *Gill's Commentary*, 6:562).

[42] According to Gill this is the "falling away" spoken of in 2 Thess 2:3: "The general defection in the times of the Papacy; when not only the eastern churches were perverted and corrupted by Mohamet, and drawn off to his religion, but the western churches were most sadly depraved by the man of sin, by bringing in errors of all sorts in doctrine, making innovations in every ordinance, and appointing new ones, and introducing both Judaism and Paganism into the churches; which general defection continued until the times of the reformation, and is what the apostle has respect to in 1 Tim. iv. 1, 2, 3" (Gill, *Gill's Commentary*, 6:575).

spiritual reign of Christ. According to some expositors the Pope took his seat in 476 AD which commenced this forty-two-month reign. But according to Gill this must be wrong because the spiritual reign had not yet begun, at least in the late 1760s. A better date for the commencement of antichrist's reign was the year 606 AD when Emperor Phocas (547–610) gave a grant of universal bishop to the Pope.[43] In addition, this is around the time Muhammed (c.570–632), the eastern antichrist, arose. Since the eastern and western antichrists begun together, they will end together. Therefore, the reign of antichrist will end around the year 1866. But Gill was uncertain of the date because Daniel's calculation of the conversion of the Jews and their reintroduction into the land was 1,290 years, that is, 3 years longer than the end of antichrist. Moreover, Daniel has given another calculation of 1,335 years when the Ottoman Empire will be destroyed and the gospel will be spread throughout the world. Consequently, according to Gill, the spiritual reign of Christ might begin sometime between 1866 to1941.[44]

Concerning the signs of this coming, as it has already been noted, Gill believed the destruction of Antichrist, the call of the Jews, the enormous conversions of Gentiles, and the spiritual reign would precede it with a period of "great coolness and indifference in religion, and great defection in faith and practice."[45] In addition, Gill maintained that "wars and rumours of wars, famines, pestilences, and earthquakes; persecutions of good men, false teachers, the preaching of the gospel throughout the world ... will be more frequent before the destruction of the world at the second coming of Christ."[46] Nevertheless, "it seems as if there would be an uncertainty of it until the sign of the Son of man, which is himself, as before observed, appears in the heavens; for the Son of man will come in an hour unthought of by good men; and as a thief in the night to wicked men; suddenly and at an unawares; and to both wise and foolish professors, whilst they are slumbering and sleeping."[47] Gill certainly did not believe in an imminent return of Christ, but he maintained that Christ's second coming could not be determined and that it would occur unexpectedly to all.[48] How then were people to prepare for this

---

[43] See Gill's comment on 2 Thess 2:8 in Gill, *Gill's Commentary*, 6:578.

[44] Gill, *Body of Divinity*, 623–624. In his sermon *The Practical Improvement of the Watchman's Answer* (1752), Gill states concerning the fulfilment of the 1260 years: "Though we can come at no certainty as to the precise time when these things shall be, yet some degree of understanding of these things may be come at; and from the circumstances of things it may be concluded, that these dates cannot reach beyond an *hundred and fifty* years more, and it may be they expire much sooner" (Gill, *Sermons and Tracts*, 1:67).

[45] Gill, *Body of Divinity*, 625.

[46] Gill, *Body of Divinity*, 624.

[47] Gill, *Body of Divinity*, 624–625.

[48] Concerning imminency Gill says in his comment on 2 Thess 2:2: "For though the coming of Christ is sometimes said to be drawing nigh and to be quickly, yet so it might be, and not at that instant: besides, such expressions are used with respect to God, with whom a thousand years are as one day, and one day as a thousand years; and because the Gospel times, or times of the Messiah, are the last days, there will be no other dispensation of things until the second coming of Christ; and chiefly they are used to keep up the

coming? Gill's answer, based on Matt 24:44 where Jesus had said, "Therefore, be ye also ready," runs thus:

> This [readiness] lies in being in Christ, having on his righteousness, and being washed in his blood; and also in regeneration and sanctification, in having true knowledge of Christ, and faith in him; for all which it becomes men to be concerned, as also all believers to be actually, as well as habitually ready; being in the lively exercise of grace, and cheerful discharge of duty, though without trusting to either.[49]

So they are to watch "in ordinances, in prayer, public and private, in hearing the word, at the Lord's Supper, and in every religious exercise; over the heart, the thoughts and affections of it; over words, actions, life, and conversation; and against all sin and unbelief, Satan's temptations, the world, and its charms and snares, false teachers and their doctrines, and for the Bridegroom's coming."[50] And why does Christ wait so long in coming? Gill states,

> The reason why he tarries is, because his time is not come, and there are many things to be done first; there is to be a glorious spread of the Gospel all over the world; all the elect must be gathered in, both Jews and Gentiles; and the man of sin must be destroyed, and the ungodly must fill up the measures of their iniquities; and Christ tarries to try the graces of his people, who should exercise faith in his coming, by looking, watching, and waiting for it, desirous of it, and hastening unto it; being ready for him, prepared to receive him, and to go with him to the nuptial-chamber.[51]

Resurrection of the dead [52]

---

faith, and awaken the hope and expectation of the saints with respect to it" (Gill, *Gill's Commentary*, 6:575).

[49] Gill, *Gill's Commentary*, 5:243.

[50] Gill, *Gill's Commentary*, 5:251. This is his comment on Matt 25:13. In the same verse he goes on to say, "This is the use and application of the whole parable, and shows the general design of it." See also his comment on 1 Thess 5:6 (Gill, *Gill's Commentary*, 6:563) and 1 John 3:3 (Gill, *Gill's Commentary*, 6:893).

[51] *Gill's Commentary*, 5:247. In 1752, Gill preached a sermon entitled, *The Practical Improvement of the Watchman's Answer* from 1 Chron 12:32 as a practical application to his sermon on prophecy entitled, *The Watchman's Answer to the Question, What of the Night?*. In *Practical Improvement*, Gill seeks to help believers know how they ought to live in light of the present time and that of the second coming. He states that "[They] ought ... to do; even *every good work*, which they should always be *ready* unto, and should pray to God to *perfect* and fit them for, and make them *fruitful* and *establish* them in" (Gill, *Sermons and Tracts*, 68) He goes on to tell them they ought "to be watchful; to strengthen the things that remain; to remember how they have received and heard, and hold fast and repent; to stand fast in the faith; to quit ye like men; to be strong; to keep close to the Word of God; to abide with the churches of Christ, and ministers of the Gospel, in the worship of God, and in the ordinances of his house; to prepare to meet their God; and to not be discouraged, for though the affliction will be sharp, it will be short" (Gill, *Sermons and Tracts*, 77–87).

[52] See Gribben, "John Gill and Puritan Eschatology," 319–320.

According to Gill, what immediately follows after the personal appearance of Christ is the resurrection of the dead. However, Gill believed that the resurrection of the just and the unjust will be separated by quite a considerable amount of time.[53] He maintained that the just would be resurrected at the time of Christ's appearance prior to the commencement of his millennial reign, and the unjust would be raised before the end of the millennium. Gill saw the former resurrection in 1 Thess 4:13–17. It, thus, coincides with the catching up of the living saints at the time of Christ's second coming.[54] Gill also identifies this resurrection as the first resurrection mentioned in Rev 20:6. Concerning the nature of the resurrected body of the righteous it will not be "a new aerial, and celestial body as Origen and others thought; or a spiritual one" but the same body although different from it "as to its qualities but not as to its substance." It will be incorruptible, immortal, "like the angels," "consist[ing] of flesh and blood," and "pure and holy."[55] Scholastically, Gill also identifies the causes of this resurrection. The efficient cause is the Father with Christ as a co-efficient cause. The meritorious cause is Christ by virtue of his death and resurrection. The instrumental cause is the voice of Christ, the sound of the of the trumpet, and the voice of the archangel. The final cause is "the glory of the grace and mercy of God, in the complete salvation of his people, soul and body."

For Gill, this doctrine was a "fundamental article of the Christian faith" because "the resurrection of Christ stands or falls with it" and "the whole gospel is connected with it and depends on it." Moreover, according to Gill, practical religion greatly depends on the truth and belief of it because it "promotes a studious concern of a holy life and conversation." It also serves to enlarge our views of such divine attributes as the omnipotence, omniscience, holiness, justice, immutability, and faithfulness. In addition, it teaches us "to think highly of Christ, as God over all" and "to endear the Spirit of God" to us. Finally, it may be "a means of encouraging our faith and trust in God, in the greatest straits and difficulties, as being able to deliver out of them" and "be of great use to support saints under the loss of near relations, 1 Thess iv. 13, 14. and under their various trials and afflictions, and under present diseases and disorders of the body."[56] The importance of this doctrine for Gill is also evident in the fact he spent answering objections to it.[57] Some of the

---

[53] For his comments on the resurrection of the dead, also see Dan 12:2–3 (Gill, *Gill's Commentary*, 4:569).

[54] See Gill, *Gill's Commentary*, 6:559–562. According to Gill, the catching up of the living saints and the raising of the dead saints occur at the same time to meet the Lord. It is interesting to note that Gill in several places calls this resurrection of living and dead saints "the rapture" of all the saints (Gill, *Gill's Commentary*, 6:561–562).

[55] For more on this resurrected body see his comments on 1 Cor 15:35–54 and 1 John 3:2.

[56] Gill, *Body of Divinity*, 602–615. Another practical application of this doctrine according to Gill is "it may direct us to a due and proper care of our bodies, whilst living, that they are not abused through avarice nor intemperance; and to provide or give orders for the descent interment of them after death" (Gill, *Body of Divinity*, 615). It should be noted that Gill preached a funeral sermon from this text for his daughter.

[57] Gill, *Body of Divinity*, 512–515. For more on the resurrection of the dead see Gill's tract entitled, *The*

details concerning the resurrection of the wicked at the end of the millennium will be given below.

Conflagration of the world
Gill believed the conflagration of the world taught in 2 Pet 3 would take place after the resurrection of the dead saints and the catching up of the living saints. Before they can descend to the earth in their new bodies the earth must be renewed.[58] This renewal is part of the restitution of all things (Acts 3:19–21), where the whole subluminary and visible world will be literally burned up.[59] This would not affect the starry heavens. This burning-up encompasses the whole earth and everything in the world.[60] All that will remain will be the pure doctrines of the Christian faith, the book of life, the covenant of grace, the word of God, the saints' title to their inheritance, their inheritance itself, and the saints themselves. Just as the bodies of the saints will be changed in quality though not in substance, so the earth will be dissolved as to its qualities but not as to its substance. It "will be only a purging, purifying, and refining it, as to its form and quality, and a removing from it every thing included in the curse, which the sin of man brought upon it; and so will become an habitation fit for the second Adam, and his holy, spiritual, and perfect offspring."[61] The most concise description of this conflagration is found in Gill's comments on 2 Peter 3:10 and 12. It will not be a melting of the four elements—earth, air, water, and fire—as the first principles are neither generated nor corrupted.[62] Rather the earth's "noxious, hurtful, unnecessary, and disagreeable things, and all the works of nature, wicked men, cattle, trees &c., and all the works of men, cities, towns, houses, furniture, utensils, instruments of arts of all sorts, will be burnt

---

Doctrine of the Resurrection, Stated and Defended in Two Sermons, in *Sermons and Tracts*, 3:335–403. In this detailed study of the resurrection of the dead Gill gives an account of those who deny this doctrine such as philosophers. He also shows that some heathen had notions of it. He then goes on to show the credibility of the resurrection and its certainty from the Scriptures. Following this Gill enquires into who shall be raised from the dead and what it is that will be raised. He proves from Scripture that the wicked will be raised, and answers objections to this truth. He also proves the immortality of the soul when answering the question of what will be raised; and he also confutes soul sleep. He goes on to prove that it is the body that died that will be raised, and then shows how the Father, Son, and Holy Spirit are involved in this resurrection. Finally, he shows the importance and use of the doctrine; it is useful for instruction and consolation.

[58] Gill believed that after Christ meets the saints in the air, he will take them to heaven while the conflagration of the earth and heavens takes place (Gill, *Gill's Commentary*, 6:562).

[59] Gill, *Body of Divinity*, 319.

[60] On 2 Pet 3:7, Gill comments that "the bodies of those that will be alive at the general conflagration will be burnt in it, though not annihilated, and will be raised again, and both soul and body will be destroyed in hell" (Gill, *Gill's Commentary*, 6:871).

[61] Gill, *Body of Divinity*, 625–636. Gill in this section also gives examples from scripture and nature to show the probability of a future conflagration, as well as answer several queries concerning it.

[62] Gill says that in 2 Pet 3:11, this includes the "sun, moon, and stars, clouds, meteors, and the fowls of the air" (Gill, *Gill's Commentary*, 6:873).

by a material fire, breaking out of the earth and descending from heaven."[63] Gill believed that in his day preparations were being made for this burning. He states:

> Witness the fiery meteors, blazing stars, and burning comets in the heavens, and the subterraneous fires in the bowels of the earth, which in some places have already broken out: there are now many volcanos, burning mountains and islands, particularly in Sicily, Italy, and the parts adjacent, the seat of the beast, and where it is very likely the universal conflagration will begin, as Aetna, Vesuvius, Strombilo, and other volcanos: and even in our own island we have some symptoms and appearances of these fires under ground, as fiery eruptions in some places, and hot waters at the Bath, and elsewhere, show; from which it is plain that the heavens and earth, that now are, are not as they always were, and will be, but are reserved and prepared for burning; and that things are ripening apace, as men's sins also are, for the general conflagration.[64]

How should Christians then live in light of this forthcoming conflagration? Gill says they should live "as men, who have their loins girt, and their lights burning, waiting for their Lord's coming; being continually in the exercise of grace, and in the discharge of their religious duties, watching, praying, hearing, reading; living soberly, righteously, and godly; guarding against intemperance and worldly-mindedness, and every worldly and hurtful lust."[65] And they should be looking for the coming of the day of God

> by faith ... look[ing] for it, and keeping looking out for it, as what will be quickly; and though it is not as soon as they desire and expect, yet should still look wistly for it, and with patience and cheerfulness wait for it: yea they should be *hasting unto* it, or *hastening* it; for though the day is fixed for the coming of Christ... yet it becomes the saints to pray earnestly for it, that it may be quickly, and for the accomplishment of all things that go before it, prepare for it, and lead unto it; such as the conversion of the Jews, and the bringing in of the fulness of the Gentiles; and by putting him in mind of and pleading with him, his promises concerning these things, and giving no rest until they are accomplished.[66]

New heavens and new earth [67]
As is taught in 2 Peter the new heavens and earth are created after the conflagration. As the conflagration will be literal, so will the new heavens and earth. The new heavens according to Gill are not the starry heavens but the airy heavens (our

---

[63] Gill, *Gill's Commentary*, 6:872.

[64] Gill, *Gill's Commentary*, 6:871.

[65] Gill, *Gill's Commentary*, 6:873.

[66] Gill, *Gill's Commentary*, 6:873.

[67] See Gribben, "John Gill and Puritan Eschatology," 320–321.

atmosphere), for the starry heavens are not burned up in the conflagration, only the airy heavens where wicked spirits fill the air. The new earth will be restored to its paradisaical estate, free from the curse. And as is depicted in Revelation 21 and 22 there will be no unbelievers, no temple, no worship as in the gospel-church-state, and no death in them, but God will dwell with his people.[68] This is the millennium of Revelation 20. Who will then live on this new earth? Gill believed that the inhabitants will be the whole general assembly and church of the firstborn, millions and millions of believers, Old and New Testament saints who are the righteous ones through Christ.[69] These ones who are inherently holy and righteous, immortal and perfect will feed on God's love in this place; God will dwell with them, and the glory of God will be upon them. This is the fulfilment of those promises of God that the saints will inherit the land (Isa 60:21; Ps 37:29; Matt 5:5).[70]

The millennium[71]
After the formation of the new heavens and earth Christ will personally reign on this new earth in "a special, peculiar, glorious, and visible kingdom."[72] Gill believed it to be "special" and "peculiar" because it would be "different from other kingdoms of Christ," that is, from Christ's kingdom of nature and providence, and from "his spiritual kingdom, which belongs to him as Mediator; which rule he had exercised in the hearts of his people from the beginning of the world."[73] According to Gill, this personal reign of Christ will last for a literal thousand years. For scripture proof of this millennial reign, Gill turned to a wide array of texts ranging from the Psalms and major prophets to the gospel writers and the book of Revelation.[74] The entirety of Old and New Testament saints will share in this kingdom and reign with Christ. This reign is to be clearly distinguished from Christ's spiritual reign since the order of civil government will be completely changed (in the latter-day glory,

---

[68] Gill maintained that there will be no need of scripture in the millennium. There will be no more need of the ministry of the word as it is now given. Because the Lamb will be the temple and light. Moreover, there will be no need to preach the gospel, since the door of faith is closed. This was the same position taken by Thomas Goodwin in *A Glimpse of Zion's Glory* (1639), see Gribben, "John Gill and Puritan Eschatology," 323.

[69] See also Gill's comment on 2 Pet 3:13, where it says, "We … look for the new heavens and a new earth wherein dwelleth righteousness." He states that "righteousness" means "righteous men; such as are so not in and of themselves, or by the deeds of the law, or by works of righteousness done by them but who are made righteous by the obedience of Christ, and are righteousness itself in him" (Gill, *Gill's Commentary*, 6:873).

[70] Gill, *Body of Divinity*, 636–642.

[71] For a detailed examination of Gill's view of the millennium, see Gribben, "John Gill and Puritan Eschatology," 321–325.

[72] Gill, *Body of Divinity*, 643.

[73] Gill, *Body of Divinity*, 643.

[74] See Pss 45, 96, 145; Isa 24:23, 30:26; Jer 23:5–6; Ezek 21:27, 48:1–35; Dan 2:44, 7:13–14; Zech 14:9; Matt 6:10, 20:21–23; Luke 1:32–33, 22:29–30; Acts 1:6; 2 Tim 4:1; Heb 2:5; and Rev 20: 1–6.

the spiritual reign of Christ, there will be no alteration in this order).[75] In addition, in this personal reign Christ will reign "with his saints" whereas in his spiritual reign, he reigns "in them." Gill describes these saints as those who have a part in the first resurrection, that is, those saints who were raised from the dead and those saints who are living at Christ's second coming. Gill further describes them as those over whom the second death has no power, and who are the priests of God and of Christ, truly blessed and holy. During these thousand years Satan will be bound and utterly unable to deceive the nations, that is, he will be unable "to draw the nations into idolatry, to fill them with bad principles, and lead them into bad practices, and to stir them to make war with the saints and persecute them." On the other hand, the saints will be in "a state of perfect purity and peace; free from being disturbed and distressed by idolaters, heretics, and persecutors." They will share in the glories of Christ's kingdom; there will be thrones and judgment for them; and they will have dominion over all their enemies, freed from sin, Satan, tribulation, the wicked, and death. At the end of thousand years Satan will be loosed and the wicked dead will be raised. They will make war against Christ and His saints and be defeated.[76] Following this will come the general judgment of the wicked.

Gill was a premillennialist. In a day when postmillennialism was on the rise and premillennialism's heyday of the seventeenth century was waning, Gill in his *Body of Divinity* continued to argue extensively for a future millennium, and answer objections to his position.

The last and general judgment[77]

Gill was convinced there was a two-fold judgment of God, one at death where a person's soul experienced happiness or woe, and the other after the resurrection of the dead. He argued for the latter with proof from reason and divine revelation.[78] The Judge will be the triune God and, in particular, the God-man Christ Jesus who will judge both angels and humans. All of humanity, good and evil, will be judged, with the former being judged first. By Gill's reckoning this judgment of the saints will take place at the beginning of the millennium after they are all raised. At that time, they will "receive the distribution of rewards, made in the kingdom state."[79] The judgment of the wicked will take place after their resurrection at the close

---

[75] Here Gill directly attacks the Fifth Monarchy movement of the seventeenth century who wanted to alter the order of civil government prior to the millennium. For Gill, this only occurs after Christ returns, raises the dead saints, burns and renews the heavens and earth and sets up his kingdom in the millennium (Gill, *Body of Divinity*, 645).

[76] Gill, *Body of Divinity*, 643–667.

[77] See Gribben, "John Gill and Puritan Eschatology," 325.

[78] His proof from reason includes: the evidence from heathen teaching; the natural conscience concerning sin and guilt; the justice of God; the relationship of the creatures to the Creator; the judgments of God in the present; and the desire of the saints after it. The proof from revelation includes Gen 4:8; 18:25; Job 19:25–26, 29; 1 Sam 2:10; Ps *passim*; Eccl 3:17; Heb 6:2; Matt 25:14–30, 31–46; Jude 24–25; and Rev 20.

[79] Gill, *Body of Divinity*, 672.

of the millennium. According to Gill's reading of scripture, the righteous and the wicked will be judged according to all their works and words, as well as thought. The rule of judgment will be according to what Gill calls the book of omniscience, the book of remembrance, the book of creation, and the book of life and other such books. According to Gill, the wicked will be "judged out of those things which are written in the books, according to their works," and the righteous

> will be judged according to their works; but not adjudged to eternal life according to them; for there is no proportion between the best works of men, and eternal life; *eternal life is the free gift of God through Christ*; but upon the judgment of them, the distribution of rewards, or of peculiar and distinguished favours, more or less, in the kingdom-state, will be according to every man's works.[80]

Gill believed that the righteous would receive rewards in the kingdom state (the millennium) but not in the eternal state. He did, however, assert that their will be degrees of punishment for the wicked in hell.[81]

Final state of the wicked in hell
After the general judgment the wicked and the righteous take their places in their final and eternal states, the wicked in hell and the righteous in heaven. According to Gill, the wicked, soul and resurrected body, will go into everlasting punishment. Again, Gill had a wide range of scriptures from which to argue his point.[82] Contrary to some divines, he maintained that Hell was not only a state but a place that goes by the names of Abaddon (destruction but not extinction), Sheol, Tophet, Gehinnon, the bottomless pit (abyss), Hades, and Tartarus. It is represented in the Bible by a number of horror-inducing images: a prison, a state of darkness, the second death, in which there is "weeping, wailing and gnashing of teeth, through grief, malice and envy."[83] For Gill, this punishment would involve both a loss of the divine presence and a sense of the wrath of God. This loss includes all good things—both God and Christ, the grace, peace and joy of the Holy Spirit as well as the holy company of angels and saints. The punishment of sense entails the body's experience of "material fire" and the soul's experience of God's wrath. Gill did not waver in his conviction that this punishment will "always continue and never have an end," a conviction he proves from various scriptures.[84] Moreover, Gill believed

---

[80] Gill, *Body of Divinity*, 675.

[81] Gill, *Body of Divinity*, 667–676.

[82] For example, the fallen angels, the flood, Sodom and Gomorrah, Korah, and the rich man in Luke 16. He also believed that it was supported from the teachings of heathens and from the human conscience.

[83] Gill, *Body of Divinity*, 681.

[84] Some of those proofs include the unquenchable fire (Matt 3:12), immortality of the soul, the impossibility of escape, and the perfections of God such as his veracity and his justice.

there would be degrees of punishment for the wicked in Hell "according to their evil works, whether more or fewer, greater or lesser."[85] The degree of punishment will depend on knowledge and actions. For example, those who have heard the gospel and been disobedient to it will aggravate their condemnation. Then the guilt and punishment for actual transgressions will be in proportion to their number and heinousness. According to Gill these degrees of punishment do not concern the punishment of loss but only of sense. Obviously, one cannot "lose more or less than another" for "all are equally excluded from the presence and communion of God and of Christ, and of the Spirit."[86]

Final state of the saints
The final state of the righteous in heaven Gill designated as a state of happiness. He argues for this from the light of nature and reason, and from divine revelation.[87] This state of happiness is variously denominated in scripture: heaven, paradise, a place of light, a house in which to dwell, a city of God's preparing, a crown of righteousness and glory, as well as glory, peace, rest, and the joy of the Lord. In this happiness, there will be freedom from all evils for both body and soul. The soul will not only be free from sin, but temptations to sin, the dominion of sin, the very being of sin, as well as the evil one, and evil men will be forever gone. The body will be free from pains and disease, hunger and thirst, and disappointment and death. From a positive angle, in this happiness, there will be the enjoyment of all that is good—God and Christ, the company of angels and saints, perfect holiness, and unending joy and felicity. As the punishment of the wicked will last forever so this happiness will never end.[88] Gill did not, however, believe that there would be degrees of blessedness in heaven. He felt that this idea of degrees in glory seemed "to incline to the popish notion" of "the merit of men," and that the scriptural proofs used for it belonged "to the kingdom-state, and not to the ultimate glory." He was assured that the arguments against degrees outweighed those for them. Some of these arguments include the fact that all of God's people are loved with the same love of God, all are chosen together in Christ, all are redeemed with Christ's

---

[85] Gill, *Body of Divinity*, 683.

[86] Gill, *Body of Divinity*, 676–686.

[87] "From the light of nature and reason: … a general notion of happiness after death … a natural desire in mankind after happiness … and the unequal distribution of things [e.g., material things and sufferings] in the present life." From divine revelation: God's promise … the predestination of men…preparation of this happiness for them … Christ's actual possession of it for His people … effectual calling of people to eternal life and happiness … the grace of God implanted in the heart and the earnest of the Holy Spirit there … the present experiences of the saints…the desires of the saints after future happiness … the assurance of it … [the beginning of it] already in this life … [and] instances of saints already in heaven [e.g., Enoch and Elijah]" (Gill, *Body of Divinity*, 686–689).

[88] The proof he offers that this happiness will never end is the Scriptural designations such as eternal life, eternal glory, house eternal in the heavens, eternal inheritance, a continuing city, everlasting kingdom, being with Christ forever, and the eternal purpose of God.

blood, and all are equally the sons of God.[89]

Gill's and Andrew Fuller's eschatology compared
James De Jong stated that at the end of the eighteenth century, Baptists followed either Gill's or Andrew Fuller's eschatology.[90] How did Fuller's eschatology differ from Gill's, and what effect did it have on Calvinistic Baptists at that time?

Fuller's eschatology differed significantly on a number of points. Most importantly, Fuller's eschatology was a postmillennialist one. He believed that Christ would come with spiritual power to inaugurate the millennium or latter-day glory.[91] At the end of this period Christ would return personally and visibly, and the resurrection of the dead, final judgment, and entrance of the saints into heaven would follow quickly upon his personal return.[92] Moreover, Fuller believed that the witnesses had already been slain and raised, that Antichrist was in the process of falling, and that the vials were being poured out in his day.[93] Fuller maintained that from the rising of the witnesses at the Reformation, and even while the vials were being poured out, the gospel would be spreading around the world.[94] He

---

[89] Gill, *Body of Divinity*, 686–694. For a similar treatment of this heavenly state see Gill's sermon, *The Glorious State of the Saints in Heaven* (1755), in *Sermons and Tracts*, 1:167–194. Two further reasons Gill gives against degrees in heaven are: all are kings and priests unto God made so by Christ; and the future glory and happiness of the saints is frequently expressed by words of the singular number (Gill, *Body of Divinity*, 693).

[90] De Jong, *As the Waters*, 202.

[91] Fuller defends his postmillennialism and "spiritual" millennium over against Gill's view of a "personal" millennium in *The Complete Works of the Rev. Andrew Fuller* (Harrisonburg, VA: Sprinkle, 1988), 1:292–293.

[92] De Jong, *As the Waters*, 202.

[93] De Jong, *As the Waters*, 204. Fuller, *Complete Works*, 1:205. Fuller believed that the first two vials had already been poured out. When he wrote his *Exposition of the Apocalypse* in 1810 or 1811, he maintained that the first vial was poured out "within the last twenty-five years" when France and the other continental powers were at war with each other. The second vial signified the wars "carrying on in the maritime nations of Spain and Portugal." The third vial had yet to be poured out but "the wars ... will ere long befall Italy and Savoy." (Fuller, *Complete Works*, 3:205). Fuller adopted Gill's interpretation of the vials (Fuller, *Complete Works*, 3:301).

[94] From the sounding of the seventh angel in Rev 11:15 at the time of the Reformation, "a signal is given of the progress of the gospel" (Fuller, *Complete Works*, 3:204). And again in Rev 14:6 after the victory over the anti-christian powers in the Reformation the angel with the everlasting gospel that comes is "the spirit lately excited to carry the gospel to the heathen" (Fuller, *Complete Works*, 3:205). In a circular letter (1810), after stating that it is not improbable that the voice of the seventh angel has begun to sound, he writes, "The glorious things spoken of the church are not all confined to the days of the millennium; many of them will go before it, in like manner as the victorious days of David went before the *rest*, or pacific reign of Solomon, and prepared its way. Previous to the fall of Babylon, an angel is seen flying in the midst of heaven, having the everlasting gospel to preach to them that dwell on the earth; and before that terrible conflict in which the beast and the false prophet are taken, the Son of God is described as riding forth on a white horse, and the armies of heaven as following him. The final ruin of the anti-christian cause will be brought upon itself by its opposition to the progress of the gospel" (Fuller, *Complete Works*, 3:363). See also his article on 'The Latter Days' where he states using Zeph 3:8 that "the universal spread of truth and of righteousness shall be preceded or accompanied by universal judgment" (Fuller, *Complete Works*, 1:642–643).

believed his day was a special time for the spread of the gospel.[95] As he wrote:

> Two hundred years have been thought to be the utmost point to which the pouring out of the vials can extend: they may terminate in less time: but if not, there is great encouragement for the friends of Christ in the promised progress of his cause *during this period*. We shall not have to wait for the Millennium, I say, ere we see glorious days in respect of the success of the gospel ... At the same time that her [church's] enemies are bleeding under the strokes of heaven, the 'kingdoms of this world are becoming the kingdoms of our Lord and of his Christ.[96]

In fact, he seems to believe that Christians could encourage the dawning of the millennium by missionary activities.[97] Thus, he expected that the millennium would come shortly.[98] Finally, Fuller did not believe it was the design of scripture prophecies to determine the exact time of the fall of antichrist. Rather he believed this fall would probably be gradual.[99]

Gill, on the other hand and as has been noted, believed that the latter-day glory would not begin until the two witnesses were slain and risen, and until antichrist, both eastern and western, had fallen at the time of the pouring out of the vials upon them. These things he thought might take place around 1866 or thereafter. For Gill, no effective spreading of the gospel to the heathen would take place until these things were fulfilled. As he stated in 1750,

> We are in the Sardinian church-state, in the latter part of it, which ... brought on the Reformation, and represents that; we are in the decline of that state: and there are many things said of that church which agree with us; as that we have a *name*, that we *live*, and are *dead*, the name of reformed churches, but without the life and power of true religion ... and yet it is not totally dark ... it is a sort of twilight with us, ... between day and night. As to what of the night is yet to come, or what will befal the churches, ... they are, the slaying of the witnesses,

---

[95] Fuller, *Complete Works*, 3:269–270, 305–306. In a circular letter (1810), he writes: "The time for the promulgation of the gospel is come; and, if attended to in a full dependence on the promise of the Spirit, it will, no doubt, be successful.—The rough places in its way are smoothing, that all flesh may see the salvation of God" (Fuller, *Complete Works*, 3:363).

[96] Fuller, *Complete Works*, 3:303–304.

[97] Fuller's friend William Carey certainly believed this, and stated so in his treatise *An Enquiry into the Obligations of Christians to Use Means for the Conversion of the Heathens* (see De Jong, *As the Waters*, 178–181). Fuller hinted at it when he says, "Had we been more importunate in prayer, we might have been more successful" (Fuller, *Complete Works*, 3:305).

[98] In 1811, he states, "We see not yet the kingdoms of this world become the kingdoms of our Lord and of his Christ; but we see that which is both preparatory and introductory to it" (Fuller, *Complete Works*, 3:301).

[99] Fuller, *Complete Works*, 3:301–302.

and the universal spread of popery all over Christendom.[100]

With regard to the universal spread of popery, he maintained:

> The papists have got ground ... But they have not as yet got the whole into their hands, as they will, and which they must, ere they can make this universal slaughter of the witnesses ... and so all churches established by the laws of the countries where they are, or all those civil and worldly establishments, are fences and guards about the witnesses: so long as these are out of the hands of the papists, they cannot come at the witnesses, they are safe; but when these are gained over, then they will be slain, and not till then. Moreover, the witnesses have not yet finished their testimony; they are still prophesying ... The slaying of the witnesses is yet to come, and will make the dismal part of that night we are entering into, and which will be accompanied with an universal spread of popery: popery will be once more the reigning, prevailing religion in Christendom.[101]

Concerning the spread of the gospel to places in the East like India, Gill stated in his comment on the sixth vial (Rev 16:12):

> To me it seems, that, through the fall of the Ottoman empire, way will be made for the kings and princes of the east, literally understood, to have and embrace the Gospel of Christ; for the Turks being destroyed, the Mahometan religion will decline, the Gospel will be carried into the eastern parts of the world into the those vast kingdoms and countries which lie in those parts, ... so that the ruin of this monarchy will pave the way for the spread of Christ's kingdom from sea to sea, and from river to river, the river Euphrates, to the ends of the earth.[102]

In light of Gill's eschatology, one can easily understand why some Gillite Baptists would consider the missionary activity of the Fullerites as an impertinent enterprise.[103] On the other hand, one can see why the Fullerites looked at the

---

[100] From the sermon *The Watchman's Answer to the Question, What of the Night?*, in *Sermons and Tracts*, 1:50–51. Gill believed that the church was presently in the Sardinian church age (the fifth church age of Rev 2–3). Gribben notes that this interpretation was a departure from the Reformation and post-Reformation interpretation of such men as John Bale (1595–1663), William Perkins (1558–1602), Johannes Cocceius (1603–1669), and Campegius Vitringa (1659–1722), who taught that the church was in the Laodicean age (Gribben, "John Gill and Puritan Eschatology," 315).

[101] Gill, *Watchman's Answer*, 52–53.

[102] Gill, *Gill's Commentary*, 6:1038–1039.

[103] I agree with De Jong that the motivation behind the anti-mission activity of some Baptists was Gillite eschatology (De Jong, *As the Waters*, 157). The response to William Carey's sermon to the Northamptonshire Association was assumed to be motivated by hyper-Calvinism. Certainly, the hyper Calvinism of some Baptists at this time would have buttressed this motivation but it was not the primary reason for it, eschatology was. Even by 1811 according to Fuller only the second vial had been poured out. Therefore, the sixth vial was

recent history of the salvation of the heathen (e.g. David Brainerd's [1718–1747] ministry in North America) as a precursor to the dawning of the millennium. There seems little doubt that eschatological conviction can have concrete influence on evangelism or missionary activity in the world. Be this as it may, eschatology needs to be in harmony with the central message of the gospel—the salvation of sinners, Jews and Gentiles. The preaching of the gospel and evangelism ought to be motivated by Matt 28:18–20, regardless of what contemporary events might appear be thought to be fulfilled.

Conclusion

After surveying Gill's eschatology and comparing it to that of Fuller, at least two unusual, if not unique, aspects of his teaching emerge. The first is his conflation of postmillennialism with premillennialism. Gill agreed with Hanserd Knollys, Daniel Whitby (1637–1726), and Jonathan Edwards (1703–1758) that there would be a period of time prior to Christ's second coming in which Christ would reign spiritually on earth called his "spiritual reign." The postmillennialists called this the "latter-day glory" or the millennial age. However, unlike them he also believed in a literal millennium after Christ's Second Coming in which Christ would personally reign on earth. Gill believed that earlier interpreters had confounded the two periods, making them one instead of two. Prior to Gill, such an interpretation does not seem to have been made in the history of eschatological thought.

A second unusual aspect has to do with Gill's date-setting of the events preceding the spiritual reign of Christ. What was unique in Gill's eschatology was his setting a date for the spiritual reign of Christ so far ahead of his day (1866, over one hundred years), joined with his belief that the fall of antichrist (eastern and western) would not take place until around that time.[104] This effectively stifled any idea of missionary endeavours to the east where the eastern antichrist still reigned. For Gillites, William Carey's idea of missions to India was overstepping God's timetable. It is true that many seventeenth-century expositors speculated on dates for Christ's return, and saw end-time events surrounding those dates. However, their dates were sufficiently close to their time that they believed the events were being fulfilled in their day. In other words, their date-setting did not hinder their obedience to spread the gospel to every creature as it did in Gill's time.[105]

still in the future in 1811. Consequently, one can see how the Gillites in the late eighteenth century would have viewed Fuller's missionary activity as presumptuous. For an article which touches on the differences between Gill's and Fuller's eschatology see W.R. Ward, "The Baptists and the Transformation of the Church, 1780–1830," *Baptist Quarterly* 25 (1973–1974): 167–175.

[104] As we have noted Gill believed they were still in the Sardinian-church state, and still needed to go through the Laodicean-church state before the fall of Antichrist would take place. The gospel would go forth in the East *after* the destruction of Antichrist, *after* the pouring out of the sixth vial (no vials had been poured out in Gill's day).

[105] It is true that there was little missionary endeavour launched from England in the seventeenth century but my point is that had there been such an endeavour I doubt that seventeenth century date setting would have hindered missions beyond England as Gill's did in the eighteenth century.

The laying aside of "empty hands": John Gill and his theology of ordination

Alex Arrell

Alex Arrell is an assistant minister at Grace Church Guildford. He grew up in Northern Ireland and worked as a solicitor for several years in London before spending some time at Capitol Hill Baptist Church in Washington, D.C., and beginning his MDiv studies through The Southern Baptist Theological Seminary in Louisville, Kentucky.

As the nation prepared to pass into a new political era, a child was born who would shape British Baptist life for the next century. Raised in a dissenting family, this self-taught boy showed enormous academic ability. Struck by a sermon he heard as an adolescent, he was later baptized and immediately began to preach. After a short spell in a small congregation, he was soon called to a London church later known around the world as the Metropolitan Tabernacle. He ministered in this prominent position until his death, after which his vast published works continued to influence Christians across the English-speaking world. In a remarkable twist of history, this record fits two men in adjacent centuries. The latter, Charles Haddon Spurgeon (1834–1892) of the nineteenth century, is well-known today. However, the first, John Gill (1697–1716) of the eighteenth century, is far less famous. This article briefly introduces this important figure, before examining one aspect of his theology, his view of ordination, more closely.

John Gill's early years (1697–1716)[1]

Born at Kettering, in Northamptonshire, on November 23, 1697, Gill's father, Edward Gill, was a deacon at the local Particular Baptist church. On the morning his son was born, a passing stranger reportedly told him that the child was to become a scholar and "all the world cannot hinder it."[2] As Gill grew up, this prediction of his potential appeared less and less dubious. Quickly surpassing his early teachers, he was sent to the local grammar school and, by the age of 11, was proficient in Latin and Greek, having read the entire Greek New Testament.[3]

Despite his development, however, it soon seemed that the world was to hinder Gill. After his schoolmaster insisted pupils attend the local Anglican church on weekdays, Gill's parents withdrew him from the school. Aware of his potential, local ministers tried to have him continue his education. However, English universities were closed to dissenters and Gill was considered too young and too academically advanced for the opportunities open to them. As a result, he was left to learn by himself. During these years, Gill demonstrated the dedication that ensured his prolific potential was realized. Until he was almost 19, he worked with his father in the woolen trade while also studying in his free time, making use of a local bookseller.[4] By this, he advanced in Greek and Latin and taught himself Hebrew, logic, rhetoric, and philosophy.[5]

These years also seen Gill develop spiritually. He came under increased conviction of sin around the age of 12 from a sermon on Genesis 3:9.[6] Although it appears Gill was converted around this time, he put off making a public profession. This was initially due to his youth. However, in later years, it was based on a realization that his church was eager to call him into pastoral ministry, which he

---

[1] The two most comprehensive biographies of Gill are undoubtedly those of his successor, John Rippon (1751–1836) and more recently by George Ella. See John Rippon, *A Brief Memoir of the Life and Writings of the Late Rev. John Gill, D.D.* (London: John Bennett, 1838), and George M. Ella, *John Gill and the Cause of God and Truth* (Eggleston, Durham: Go Publications, 1995). However, it should be noted that Ella's work is openly polemical, attempting to vindicate Gill's ministry and theology from various allegations that have been made against him. Helpful shorter historical treatments can be found in the anonymous account of his life later prefaced to his works and the chapter by Charles Spurgeon. John Gill, *A Collection of Sermons and Tracts* (London: George Keith, 1773), C.H. Spurgeon, *The Metropolitan Tabernacle: Its History and Work* (London: Passmore & Alabaster, 1876). More recent short accounts of his life by Timothy George, Robert Oliver, and Tom Nettles are also instructive, see Timothy George, "John Gill," in *Theologians of the Baptist Tradition*, ed. Timothy George and David S. Dockery, rev. ed. (Nashville, TN: B&H, 2001); Robert W. Oliver, "John Gill (1697–1771): His Life and Ministry," in *The Life and Thought of John Gill (1697–1771): A Tercentennial Appreciation*, ed. Michael A.G. Haykin (Leiden: Brill, 1997), 7–50; Thomas J. Nettles, *By His Grace and For His Glory: A Historical, Theological and Practical Study of the Doctrines of Grace in Baptist Life* (Cape Coral, FL: Founders, 2006).

[2] Even prior to his birth, Gill's father was convinced that he was to have a son who would become famous among such churches. Ella, *John Gill and the Cause of God and Truth*, 38–39.

[3] George, "John Gill," 13.

[4] John Gill, *A Collection of Sermons and Tracts* (London: George Keith, 1773), 1:xi.

[5] Rippon, *Brief Memoir*, 5.

[6] Gill, *Collection of Sermons and Tracts*, 1:xii.

did not feel ready for.[7] It was only after years of preparing for such ministry that Gill publicly professed his faith on November 1, 1716, and was baptized the same day.[8] Three days later he partook of the Lord's Supper for the first time and, at a prayer gathering in a private home that evening, read and expounded on Isaiah 53. As expected, Gill was quickly pressed towards public ministry, being asked to preach the following Sunday evening.[9]

Gill's ministry years (1717–1771)
From 1717 to 1719, Gill assisted pastors in Particular Baptist churches at Kettering and nearby market town Higham-Ferrers.[10] During this time, he also met Elizabeth Negus (1696–1764). They married in 1718 and had a devoted life together until Elizabeth's death.[11] While they had multiple children, only three survived infancy.[12] The death of his daughter, also named Elizabeth, at the age of 13 in 1738 resulted in one of Gill's most hope-filled and heartfelt funeral sermons.[13]

In early 1719, Benjamin Stinton (1677–1719), the son-in-law and pastoral successor to Benjamin Keach (1640–1704) at Horselydown in London, died. Gill preached several times for the church and, after being called by the congregation, was ordained as their pastor on March 22, 1720. Serving them for the next 51 years, he was only to relinquish the role upon his death on October 14, 1771.

Gill faced several church disputes and divisions during his first three years, and in 1723 almost died after becoming severally ill. However, from 1724, his ministry began to ripen and expand. This was the year that Gill published his first work, a funeral sermon, and began a much-celebrated preaching series through the Song of Solomon, which lasted for 122 sermons. From 1726, he began to publicly engage

---

[7] George, "John Gill," 13.

[8] His ability was again evident from this early stage, with the gathering singing a baptismal hymn that he had written for the occasion of his own baptism. Gill, *Collection of Sermons and Tracts*, 1:xii.

[9] Gill, *Collection of Sermons and Tracts*, 1:xiii.

[10] Rippon, *Brief Memoir*, 10–11. It was during these years that Gill was one of the first beneficiaries who received a financial grant from the relatively new Particular Baptist Fund. He would also later receive further finances to purchase some of John Skepp's (d. 1721) Hebrew books, making good use of them in expanding his expertise. Spurgeon, *Metropolitan Tabernacle*, 40–41. Gill became a manager of the Fund only a few years later in 1724. B.R. White, "John Gill in London (1719-1729): A Biographical Fragment," *Baptist Quarterly* 22 (1968–1967): 81.

[11] Sharon James, "'The Weaker Vessel': John's Gill's Reflections on Women, Marriage and Divorce," in *Life and Thought of John Gill*, 216–218.

[12] Oliver, "John Gill (1697–1771): His Life and Ministry," 42–43.

[13] At the beginning of this sermon, Gill reflected: "So hard a thing is it for us to keep the doctrines of the gospel always in view; and harder still to make use of them, and live up to them, when we most want them. What can have a greater tendency to moderate our trouble, which naturally arises from the departure of our dearest friends, than to consider, that they are laid down to rest for a while; that they are asleep, and asleep in the arms of Jesus; that they will awake in the morning of the resurrection fresh and chearful; that Christ will bring them with him at his second coming, when we shall meet together again, and never part more, but *shall be for ever with the Lord?*" (Gill, *Collection of Sermons and Tracts*, 1:391).

in theological disputes, the first two being with Independents over baptism and with Deists on the Old Testament. By 1729 he was seen as a leader beyond his own church and denomination, being invited to lecture on a weeknight to a wider audience. He did so for the next 27 years, later using these lectures for his many treatises and commentaries.[14]

Over the next four decades, Gill produced a steady stream of work, publishing more than ten thousand pages and receiving the nickname "Dr. Voluminous" as a result.[15] He was not only the first Baptist to produce a complete systematic theology, but he was also the first to write a commentary on the whole Bible. This nine-volume work was widely used across the English-speaking world for the next century.[16] In 1748, Gill was surprised to receive a Doctor of Divinity from Aberdeen University on account of his recently published commentary on the New Testament, as well as his "honest and learned defence … against the profane attacks of Deists and Infidels."[17] As a result, despite the difficulties of being a dissenter, Gill was recognized as a scholar, just as it was predicted.

Gill's legacy[18]

While few have questioned the extent of Gill's pen, the effect of his pastoring has regularly been criticized. Even the normally sympathetic Spurgeon views him as affectionate, yet aloof.[19] He also suggests membership declined significantly in Gill's final years, with him refusing to relinquish control over the congregation.[20] However, the size of the membership in these years is difficult to determine, and despite the widespread decline of Particular Baptist churches, it is notable that the congregation likely remained the largest in London.[21]

[14] Gill, *Collection of Sermons and Tracts*, 1:xviii.

[15] George, "John Gill," 12.

[16] Spurgeon later commented, "Many sneer at Gill, but he is not to be dispensed with. In some respects, he has no superior. He is always well worth consulting" (C.H. Spurgeon, *C.H. Spurgeon's Autobiography, Compiled from His Diary, Letters, and Records, by His Wife and His Private Secretary, 1834-1854*) (Cincinnati, OH: Curts & Jennings, 1898), 1:255.

[17] Rippon, *Brief Memoir*, 58.

[18] For recent brief examinations of Gill's theology, see Timothy George's and Tom Nettles's works. For a fuller analysis, see *Life and Thought of John Gill (1697–1771)*, edited by Michael A.G. Haykin. Also see David Mark Rathel, "Was John Gill a Hyper-Calvinist? Determining Gill's Theological Identity," *Baptist Quarterly* 48.1 (2017): 47–59; Rathel, "John Gill and the History of Redemption as Mere Shadow: Exploring John Gill's Doctrine of the Covenant of Redemption," *Journal of Reformed Theology* 4.11 (2017): 477–400; Rathel, "A Case Study in Baptist Catholicity: The Scriptures and the Tradition in the Theology of John Gill," *Baptist Quarterly* 49.3 (2018): 1–9.

[19] Spurgeon, *Metropolitan Tabernacle*, 42–43.

[20] Spurgeon, *Metropolitan Tabernacle*, 45–46.

[21] On the decline of Particular Baptists in England, Michael A.G. Haykin points out that "in 1715, for instance, there were around 220 Particular Baptist churches in England and Wales. By 1750 the number had shrunk to about 150" (Haykin, "Introduction," in *Life and Thought of John Gill*, 1). Also see Haykin, *Ardent Love for Jesus: Learning from the Eighteenth-Century Baptist Revival* (Bryntirion, Bridgend: Bryntirion,

Even more than allegations of an underwhelming pastoral ministry, it is accusations of antinomianism and high Calvinism that have done the greatest damage to Gill's reputation.[22] Far from being perceived as the preserver of Particular Baptist churches in these years, Gill has been portrayed as their polluter, securing rather than slowing their decline.[23] Historically, most have concluded, along with H. Leon McBeth, that Gill's high Calvinism, and his resulting "non-invitational" preaching, "brought the kiss of death to Particular Baptists."[24] However, more recent assessments by Tom Nettles and Timothy George challenge this conclusion.[25] George argues that Gill has often been judged by the flaws of his followers and friends, and through the lens of their later dispute with Andrew Fuller (1754–1815), rather than being assessed in his own words and context.[26] This is perhaps what Spurgeon suggests when he calls for Gill's critics to consider him more closely, arguing Gill actually said many things that diverged from high Calvinism.[27]

2013). For an overview of the difficulty of estimating the size of the membership, see Oliver, "John Gill," 41. Spurgeon claims that by Gill's death, the church barely numbered 150 members (Spurgeon, *Metropolitan Tabernacle*, 46). However, as Ella points out, no more than 150 members were active when Gill became pastor. Further, though he perhaps attracted many hearers, the membership did not expand significantly. For example, in 1757 there were around 235 members. Despite this relatively modest increase, the congregation was considered the largest Particular Baptist church in London during Gill's ministry, with such churches only having an average of 50 members in 1753 (Ella, *John Gill and the Cause of God and Truth*, 62–63). The fact that there was a substantial exodus from the church upon Gill's death, leaving Rippon with only 90 members upon his arrival, only strengthens the case that Gill was still attracting members even at the end of his ministry.

Gill tried to establish a successor on several occasions, even offering to resign, but the congregation refused to relinquish him, insisting that he remained as pastor until his death. Further, from 1770 Gill attempted several times to have the church appoint Benjamin Francis as his successor and, in April 1771, even offered to resign to allow the congregation to be better cared for given his increasing infirmities (Ella, *John Gill and the Cause of God and Truth*, 239–240).

[22] For example, as part of its short description, William H. Brackney states: "Gill became known for his extreme Calvinism, 'unable to offer Christ to sinners because it did not respect the sovereignty of God.' His ministry concentrated on the edification of an elect church" (William H. Brackney, *Historical Dictionary of the Baptists* [Lanham, MD: Scarecrow, 2009], 251). Such a conclusion appears to have been popularized soon after his death, with the infamous statement of Robert Hall, Jr. (1764–1831) on Gill's *Body of Doctrinal and Practical Divinity* being that it was "a continent of mud" (James Leo Garrett, Jr., *Baptist Theology: A Four-Century Study* [Macon, GA: Mercer University Press, 2009], 104).

[23] In contrast, Haykin points out that there is a more multifaceted explanation for this decline, including the influence of political, social, and geographic factors (Haykin, "Introduction," 1).

[24] Haykin, "Introduction," 3.

[25] George, "John Gill," 24–29; Nettles, *By His Grace and For His Glory*, 76–106.

[26] George, "John Gill," 29. Garrett agrees by suggesting "more negative assessments have come chiefly from historians of the Baptists who have related Gill to the spiritual decline of the Particular Baptists of his day, whereas the more positive assessments have been given by theologians who have majored on extensive reading of Gill's writings" (Garrett, *Baptist Theology: A Four-Century Study*, 104).

[27] "The system of theology with which many identify his name has chilled many churches to their very soul, for it has led them to omit the free invitations of the gospel, and to deny that it is the duty of sinners to

In the end, whether Gill was a Hyper-Calvinist or not entirely depends on how that term is defined.[28] By most definitions, there are aspects of his theology that tend towards it, especially his support for eternal justification.[29] Nevertheless, we must be careful not to treat the seeds of a theology as the fully formed system itself. Notwithstanding the logical implications of his views, Gill persistently and publicly opposed antinomianism.[30] Further, as explored in more detail below, he understood and explicitly called for pastors to be "instrumental in the conversion of sinners."[31] Indeed, Gill modelled this in his ministry, for he was unafraid to address sinners in his sermons and regularly witnessed conversions.[32] While Gill "was no [George] Whitefield [1714–1770]," and could be criticized for failing to engage with the evangelistic emphases of the Evangelical Revival, this task fell to the next generation of Particular Baptists, to whom Gill should be seen more as a help than a hindrance.[33]

---

believe in Jesus: but for this Dr. Gill must not be altogether held responsible, for a candid reader of his commentary will soon perceive in it expressions altogether out of accord with such a narrow system; and it is well known that when he was dealing with practical godliness he was so bold in his utterances that the devotees of Hyper-Calvinism could not endure him" (Spurgeon, *Metropolitan Tabernacle*, 47).

[28] For example, Garrett understands high Calvinism to comprise of five teachings: supralapsarianism, covenant of redemption, eternal justification, no general offers of grace, and antinomianism. As a result, he argues Gill is "reasonably described either as three-fifths or as four-fifths a Hyper-Calvinist, he not being an antinomian and being ambiguous on supralapsarianism" (Garrett, *Baptist Theology*, 100). However, many would disagree with parts of this definition, particularly the inclusion of a covenant of redemption as an aspect of Hyper-Calvinism. A more nuanced and accurate analysis is that of Michael A.G. Haykin, "Hyper-Calvinism and the Theology of John Gill" (paper presented at the True Church Conference, Muscle Shoals, AL, February 2010), 1–16.

[29] Haykin, "Hyper-Calvinism and the Theology of John Gill," 12–14.

[30] Garrett, *Baptist Theology*, 99–100.

[31] Gill asserted this at the ordination service of George Braithwaite (1681–1748) (Gill, *Collection of Sermons and Tracts*, 2:13). Ken Manley also points out that the pastoral successor Gill asked his deacons to appoint, Benjamin Francis (1734–1799), was known to favor a direct evangelistic appeal, see Ken R. Manley, *"Redeeming Love Proclaim": John Rippon and the Baptists* (Eugene, OR: Wipf and Stock, 2004), 35.

[32] Ella, *John Gill and the Cause of God and Truth*, 51, 246. At the conclusion of a particularly moving funeral sermon for John Smith, Gill reflects: "What encouragement is here for poor sinners from hence to hope for grace and mercy through Christ? What though, poor soul, thou seest the aboundings of sin in thy nature, and in every power and faculty of thy soul; yet look up and view the superabounding grace of God streaming through the person, blood, and righteousness of Christ; it is a mercy that thou seest the plague of thine own heart, and art not left to thy native blindness, to a vain conceit of the goodness of thy estate, when thou wert poor, wretched, miserable, and blind and naked; take heart, therefore, and do not be discouraged; Christ's grace is sufficient for thee; and where sin abounded, grace hath much more so; there is enough in Christ for thee; there is righteousness to clothe, and bread to nourish, grace to sanctify, strength to support, and every thing needful for thee; go to him as a poor perishing sinner, implore his grace, and venture on him, I dare say he will not reject thee" (Gill, *Collection of Sermons and Tracts*, 1:350).

[33] Even if Gill did not help the progress of the Particular Baptists towards great evangelistic expansions, he protected and prepared them for this work in the next generation. This is also Haykin's assessment, who admits that although "Gill's theology did hamper passionate evangelism and outreach," asserts that his "fidelity gave form and shape to the coals of orthodoxy upon which the fire of revival fell later in the century through men like Andrew Fuller, John Ryland, Jr., and William Carey" (Haykin, "Hyper-Calvinism and the

It is unfortunate that controversy over Gill's Calvinism has overshadowed his conflicts with Deists and Socinians, through which Particular Baptists were spared the theological developments that would decimate the General Baptists and Presbyterians.[34] Nevertheless, it is unsurprising that Gill's soteriology shaped his legacy, for he set it at the center of his ministry. Gill devoted many of his most protracted works and public disputes to such subjects, including the four volumes of *The Cause of God and Truth*, responding to what many considered to be Daniel Whitby's (1638–1726) unanswerable arguments for Arminianism, and several treatises against John Wesley (1703–1791) over the doctrines of perseverance and predestination. Further, it can be argued that it is a single soteriological theme that permeates Gill's entire corpus, which is "grace and glory." The comprehensive nature of God's grace in salvation, and its certain causation of future glory, was a theme that even "Dr. Voluminous" seemed unable to exhaust.[35]

Given the controversy over Gill's legacy, there is a danger of perceiving him to be a cold and combative doctrinarian. However, while he was often polemical, he was also practical. Indeed, the peak of his greatest project was arguably the production of his *Body of Practical Divinity*, which was his last published work.[36] It had taken him decades to get to this part of the project. The first volume of his commentary was published in 1746, with the last finally finished in 1766. Based on

---

Theology of John Gill," 16).

[34] Nettles, *By His Grace and For His Glory*, 73. Thankfully it appears that increasing attention has been given to the importance and impact of Gill's orthodoxy. For example, Steven Godet defends the thesis that "Gill's formulation and defence of the doctrine of the Trinity was faithful to the Scriptures and vital to the preservation of orthodox trinitarianism among Particular Baptists in the long eighteenth century" (Steven Tshombe Godet, "The Trinitarian Theology of John Gill [1697–1771]: Context, Sources, and Controversy" [PhD diss., The Southern Baptist Theological Seminary, 2015], 9).

[35] For example, in his preaching Gill comments: God made a covenant with his people in Christ "to give them grace and glory" (Gill, *Collection of Sermons and Tracts*, 1:3); it is *"eternal glory*, the God of all grace calls his people to, and will put them in the possession of" (Gill, *Collection of Sermons and Tracts*, 1:114); "God first gives grace, and then gives glory; and to whomsoever he gives the one, he gives the other" (Gill, *Collection of Sermons and Tracts*, 1:120); "God gives glory to none but to whom he first gives grace; grace is his first gift, and glory is his last; and none have the latter, but those who share in the former" (Gill, *Collection of Sermons and Tracts*, 1:121); in Christ there are "immense treasures of grace and glory which lie hid in his person" (Gill, *Collection of Sermons and Tracts*, 1:147–148); the elect will be "filled with grace, and made meet for glory" (Gill, *Collection of Sermons and Tracts*, 1:183), because the elect are in Christ's person "their grace being there, it can never be lost; their glory being there, they can never be deprived of it … Their life, both of grace and glory, is hid with Christ in God, and so out of the reach of men and devils … Christ is the storehouse and magazine of all grace and glory, and a well fortified one; he is a rock, a strong tower, a place of defence, such an one as the gates of hell cannot prevail against" (Gill, *Collection of Sermons and Tracts*, 1:183); "none shall reign with Christ in glory, but those in whose hearts grace has reigned here" (Gill, *Collection of Sermons and Tracts*, 1:351). Indeed, Gill's understanding of this majestic theme is well summarized by his declaration in a sermon that, "there is an inseparable connection between the blessings of grace, and eternal glory; to whom he gives the one he gives the other; whom he did predestinate, them he also called; and whom he called, them he also justified; and whom he justified, them he also glorified" (Gill, *Collection of Sermons and Tracts*, 1:166). Similar references can be found not only throughout the rest of Gill's preaching, but also in his theological and exegetical works.

[36] Rippon, *Brief Memoir*, 99.

his exposition of the whole canon, Gill published a *Body of Doctrinal Divinity* in 1769. In 1770, the year before his death, his *Body of Practical Divinity* was produced in order to complete his life's project.[37] As the pinnacle of his piety, this includes a whole book on the practical worship of God, bringing Gill's doctrinal foundations to their devotional fulfilment. In this, he spends 24 chapters contemplating the meaning and means of true heart worship, and develops an understanding of godliness that is well summarized as "the Godward soul." Being both rigorous and rich, this work is perhaps Gill at his very best.

Having introduced Gill, this essay now examines his theology of ordination in its context, arguing that it had a slow, yet significant, impact on later Particular Baptist practices.

Particular Baptist ordination (1644–1697)
In 1644, leaders of seven Particular Baptist congregations in London published the First London Confession to defend themselves from allegations of doctrinal error and distinguish their theology from that of the Anabaptists and General Baptists.[38] However, on appointing pastors and deacons, the First London Confession is substantially less specific than the earliest Arminian or General Baptist documents.[39] Later Particular Baptist confessions included a much fuller treatment. The Somerset Confession (1656) was the first Particular Baptist confession to mention ordination.[40] Most importantly, the Second London Confession (1677/1688) continued this trend, largely taking its language from the

---

[37] Gill himself explains the connection between the many decades of his exegetical and theological work in this way: "Having completed an exposition of the whole Bible, the books both of the Old and of the New Testament, I considered with myself what would be best next to engage in for the further instruction of the people under my care; and my thoughts led me to enter upon a scheme of Doctrinal and Practical Divinity, first the former and then the latter; the one being the foundation of the other, and both having a close connexion with each other" (John Gill, *A Complete Body of Doctrinal and Practical Divinity: Or A System of Evangelical Truths, Deduced from the Sacred Scriptures* (London: Tegg & Company, 1839), 1:vii.

[38] W.J. McGlothlin, *Baptist Confessions of Faith* (Philadelphia: American Baptist Publication Society, 1911), 168.

[39] Article XXXVI briefly states that "every Church has power given them from Christ for their better well-being, to choose to themselves meet persons into the office of Pastors, Teachers, Elders, Deacons" (McGlothlin, *Baptist Confessions of Faith*, 184). For example, the 38 Dutch articles signed by John Smyth (c.1554–c.1612) and others prior to August 1612, stated in Articles 25 and 26 that "the vocation or election of the said officers is performed by the church, with fasting, and prayer to God … And although the election and vocation to the said offices is performed by the aforesaid means, yet, nevertheless, the investing into the said service is accomplished by the elders of the church through the laying on of hands" (McGlothlin, *Baptist Confessions of Faith*, 61). Similarly, the *General Baptist Confession* in 1651 states in Article 73 that "Fasting and Prayer ought to be used, and laying on of hands, for the Ordaining of servants or Officers to attend about the service of God" (McGlothlin, *Baptist Confessions of Faith*, 107).

[40] G. Hugh Wamble, "Baptist Ordination practices to 1845," *Baptist History & Heritage* 23.3 (1988): 17. It states in Article XXXI: "the church of Jesus Christ with its ministry may from among themselves, make choice of such members, as are fitly gifted and qualified by Christ, and approve and ordain such by fasting, prayer, and laying on of hands (Acts 13:3; 14:23)" (McGlothlin, *Baptist Confessions of Faith*, 211).

Savoy Declaration (1658).⁴¹ Article nine of chapter XXVI holds:

> The way appointed by Christ for the Calling of any person, fitted, and gifted by the Holy Spirit, unto the Office of Bishop, or Elder, in a Church, is, that he be chosen thereunto by the common suffrage of the Church itself; and Solemnly set apart by Fasting and Prayer, with imposition of hands of the Eldership of the Church, if there be any before Constituted therein; And of a Deacon that he be chosen by the like suffrage, and set apart by Prayer, and the like Imposition of hands.⁴²

This view was widely accepted by Particular Baptists for the rest of the seventeenth and early eighteenth centuries.⁴³ For example, Keach, a leading signatory, reflected

---

⁴¹ Most directly from Article XI in *Of The Institution Of Churches, And The Order Appointed In Them By Jesus Christ* found at the end of the Savoy Declaration. See Philip Schaff, ed., *The Creeds of Christendom, with a History and Critical Notes: The Evangelical Protestant Creeds, with Translations* (New York: Harper & Brothers, 1882), 725. However, the Second London Confession does not include the following two clarifying statements that the Savoy Declaration later went on to make in Articles XII and XV: "The Essence of this Call of a Pastor, Teacher, or Elder unto Office consists in the Election of the Church, together with his acceptation of it, and separation by Fasting and Prayer: And those who are so chosen, though not set apart by Imposition of Hands, are rightly constituted Ministers of Jesus Christ … Ordination alone, without the Election or precedent consent of the Church, by those who formerly have been Ordained by virtue of that Power they have received by their Ordination, doth not constitute any person a Church-Officer, or communicate Office-power unto him" (Schaff, ed., *Creeds of Christendom*, 3:725–726). Wamble suggests that these were likely excluded from the Second London Confession in the interest of brevity, as opposed to any disagreement with them (Wamble, "Baptist Ordination Practices to 1845," 18).

⁴² McGlothlin, *Baptist Confessions of Faith*, 266.

⁴³ Joseph Ivimey records that thirteen London churches, including Horselydown, formed an association in 1704 and explains that "it had frequently been a subject of controversy in the denomination, whether the laying on of hands upon ministers at their ordination was proper or necessary. Some churches not only pleased strenuously for this practice, as an apostolic and primitive custom; but also contended for the necessity of laying on the hands of pastors upon deacons when elected to that office as well as upon person who had been baptized, introducing them into the church by this rite." Ivimey notes while the association gave no opinion on the latter practice, leaving room for different opinions among the churches, it concluded "the ordination of persons to the office of an elder, or that of a deacon, by the imposition of the hands of the eldership, is an ordinance of Jesus Christ still in force" (Joseph Ivimey, *A History of the English Baptists* [London: B.J. Holdsworth, 1823], 3:56–57). Wamble also points out that the London Association took the lead in encouraging the practice of public ordination by even financing London ministers to travel to ordain ministers elsewhere (Wamble, "Baptist Ordination Practices to 1845," 18).

Similarly, Ivimey states that an association of churches in the west of England met in 1653 and records there being debate and disagreement over the imposition of hands on baptized believers more generally, but unanimous agreement that ordination should be accompanied by the laying on of hands (Joseph Ivimey, *A History of the English Baptists*, [London: Isaac Taylor Hinton and Holdsworth & Ball, 1830], 4:257]. Other correspondence from the same association only a few years later stated that there was eventually debate over the imposition of hands in ordination, with messengers from five churches questioning it. However, they were not opposed to the use of it and so the majority of the messengers decided to proceed anyway with the practice (Ivimey, *A History of the English Baptists*, 4:292–293).

There was not only a lack of opposition to these practices, but there was also positive assertion of them. Ernest A. Payne points out that the leading London Baptist minister, Hercules Collins (1646–1702), argued in 1702 that ordination was "a gospel ordinance" and told his readers to "never part with that Rite and

the same position in the condensed version he had his church ratify as their confession in 1697.[44] In his appendix to that document, Keach reinforced this view of ordination, stating: "A Church thus constituted ought forthwith to choose them a Pastor, Elder or Elders, and Deacons … Moreover, they are to take special care, … after in a Day of solemn Prayer and Fasting, that they have elected them, (whether Pastor, &c., or Deacons) and they accepting the Office, must be ordained with Prayer, and laying on of Hands of the Eldership."[45] However, it also should be noted that Keach had an expanded view of the imposition of hands, meaning that he practiced it not only at ordination, but also on every baptized believer.[46] One of the key differences between Keach's confession and the Second London Confession is the addition of an article on this point.[47] This position not only reflected that of his predecessor, William Rider (1723–1785), but was also retained by his pastoral successor, Benjamin Stinton.[48]

The standard ordination service

The view of ordination outlined by Keach and the Second London Confession in the seventeenth century shaped practice throughout the eighteenth century. While flexibility always remained, Nigel Wheeler has shown that ordination followed a consistent procedure.[49] After a congregation called a candidate, and upon his

---

Ceremony in Ordination of Imposition of Hands, with Prayer, on the Person ordained" (Ernest A. Payne, "Baptists and the Laying on of Hands," *Baptist Quarterly* 15 [1954]: 204).

[44] McGlothlin, *Baptist Confessions of Faith*, 289–90. In Article XXV, Keach stated: "said Elders and Deacons so chosen, ought solemnly to be ordained with Prayer, and laying on of Hands of the Eldership" (Benjamin Keach, *A Short Confession of Faith Containing the Substance of All the Fundamental Articles in the Larger Confession Put Forth by the Elders of the Baptist Churches, Owning Personal Election and Final Perseverance* [London, 1697]).

[45] Benjamin Keach, *The Glory of a True Church, and Its Discipline Display'd Wherein a True Gospel-Church is Described: Together with the Power of the Keys, and Who are to Be Let in, and Who to Be Shut Out* (London, 1697), 8.

[46] Parratt, "Early Baptist on the Laying on of Hands," 325–27.

[47] Article XXIII specifies that "laying on of Hands (with Prayer) upon baptized Believers, as such, is an Ordinance of Christ, and ought to be submitted unto by all such Persons that are admitted to partake of the Lord's Supper" (Keach, *Short Confession of Faith*). James Vaughn argues that Keach also had "a very high evaluation of the status and authority of the ministry." Further he made a possible implication of the *Second London Confession* explicit by arguing that only an ordained minister could administer baptism and the Lord's Supper. This reflected the "sharp distinction" he made between lay and ordained, which "implied that the ordained have a higher status than lay church members" (James Barry Vaughn, "Public Worship and Practical Theology in the Work of Benjamin Keach [1640-1704]" [PhD thesis, University of St. Andrews, 1989], 325).

[48] Spurgeon, *Metropolitan Tabernacle*, 17, 58.

[49] Nigel David Wheeler, "Eminent Spirituality and Eminent Usefulness: Andrew Fuller's (1754–1815) Pastoral Theology in His Ordination Sermons" (PhD diss., University of Pretoria, 2009), 82. Also see Wheeler, *The Pastoral Priorities of 18th Century Baptists: An Examination of Andrew Fuller's Ordination Sermons* (Peterborough, ON: H&E, 2021). Although Wheeler's research draws heavily from sources in the late eighteenth century, earlier sources suggest that the procedure generally remained unchanged throughout the

acceptance, surrounding pastors were invited to preside over the ordination at a special service.[50] In addition to scripture readings, prayers and singing, this lengthy service contained four separate discourses: the introductory discourse, the ordinand's statement of faith, the charge to the new pastor, and the pastoral address to the Church.[51]

Wheeler suggests that the moment of ordination came after the first two discourses, taking place through an ordination prayer. During this, visiting ministers would lay their hands on the ordinand.[52] While only a few ministers would preach or pray at the service, all in attendance would join together in this imposition of hands.[53] If deacons were also being ordained, a separate prayer and imposition of hands was included for them in the service.[54]

The ordination of John Gill (1720)

Given Keach's views, it is unsurprising that when his Horselydown congregation later elected Gill, the process largely proceeded as above. However, from this we should not conclude that Gill's ordination was uncontroversial. Indeed, immediately after his election, disagreements over his appointment divided the church and the majority, who selected Gill, were temporarily removed from their meetinghouse.[55] Reflecting on these events, George comments, "Gill's call to the Horselydown church has all the drama of an ecclesiastical soap opera."[56] Nevertheless, when the service finally took place, it followed the usual pattern.[57] After the church met privately for prayer, a public service involving no less than ten visiting ministers

---

century. For example, Stinton was involved in a very similar service for the ordination of Joseph Burroughs in 1717 (Ivimey, *History of the English Baptists*, 3:148–149).

[50] Wheeler suggests they believed inviting surrounding ministers was necessary as only elders could ordain an elder. The service often took place midweek, and while it normally lasted from three to four hours, it could go on longer (Wheeler, "Eminent Spirituality and Eminent Usefulness," 84–87).

[51] Wheeler, "Eminent Spirituality and Eminent Usefulness," 94.

[52] The ordination prayer was intended to plead for God's blessing upon the relationship between the congregation and the new minister. See Wheeler, "Eminent Spirituality and Eminent Usefulness," 109–110.

[53] Wheeler, "Eminent Spirituality and Eminent Usefulness," 85. As all of the above confessions make clear, Particular Baptists held that the church alone selected its officers. Nevertheless, they also generally believed it was the visiting ministers who had the right to lay hands on an ordinand. Although it was acknowledged that ultimately this authority was given to them by the church through the invitation from the congregation to ordain the pastor (Wheeler, "Eminent Spirituality and Eminent Usefulness," 109).

[54] Wheeler, "Eminent Spirituality and Eminent Usefulness," 116.

[55] While Gill accepted the church's call on September 20, 1719, these complications meant his ordination did not occur until March 22, 1720. Gill ministered to the church during part of this period, although it appears other ministers attended services when necessary to administer the Lord's Supper to the congregation. See Ella, *John Gill and the Cause of God and Truth*, 44–54.

[56] George, "John Gill," 14.

[57] A fuller record can be found in Rippon, *Brief Memoir*, 12–14.

was held.[58] At the moment of ordination itself, the record explains:

> The Rev. Mr. [John] Curtis, and the aged and Rev. Mr. Mark Key [d. 1726], then pastor of the church near Devonshire-square, were appointed to take the lead in the distinctive part of ordination—and the excellent man "was ordained by laying on of hands." Three brethren also were immediately "ordained and set apart" to the office of deacons, "Mr. Gill joining with the other elders in the imposition of hands."[59]

The ordination sermons of John Gill

The ordination of those three deacons at Horselydown was the first of many for Gill. Spurgeon reflects, "the ordination discourses and funeral sermons which he preached must have amounted to a very large number: it seemed as if no Particular Baptist minister could be properly inducted or interred without Dr. Gill's officiating."[60] Of these, four of Gill's charges to newly ordained pastors have been preserved and published, being those given to: (1) George Braithwaite at the meeting-house near Devonshire-Square on March 28, 1734; (2) Gill's nephew, also called John Gill (d. 1809), at St. Albans on June 7, 1758; (3) John Davis at Waltham-Abbey on August 15, 1764; and (4) John Reynolds at Curriers' Hall near Cripple-Gate on October 2, 1766.[61] Surveying these sermons reveals much about Gill's concept of the office into which they were ordained.

Of the four, the charge given to John Davis in 1764 stands apart, with Gill preaching from the seemingly obscure text of Ezekiel 10:20.[62] In using this text to trace "the qualifications, duties, work, and usefulness of the ministers of the gospel," Gill demonstrated his command of the biblical canon, drawing together references and illusions from across scripture in order to argue cherubim are neither divine persons nor angelic beings, but are rather ministers of the gospel. While his hearers may have been somewhat surprised at the subject, the sermon provides a powerful

---

[58] Ella, *John Gill and the Cause of God and Truth*, 53.

[59] Rippon, *Brief Memoir*, 12–13.

[60] Spurgeon, *Metropolitan Tabernacle*, 39. Four examples of such ordination sermons can be found in Gill, *Collection of Sermons and Tracts*, 2:1–64.

[61] Gill, *Collection of Sermons and Tracts*, 2:1, 14, 30, 49. For further details of these services, see Joseph Ivimey, *A History of the English Baptists* (London: Ivimey, 1814), 2:176, and Ivimey, *History of the English Baptists*, 4:321–22. The published charge from the ordination of John Gill also notes that four others, James Larwill, Isaac Gould, Bonner Stone, and Walter Richards, were ordained at the same time, likely as deacons in the church alongside their new pastor.

[62] Gill, *Collection of Sermons and Tracts*, 2:30. Gill was not unaware of this apparent oddity, for he asserts at the very beginning of his message, "It may seem strange to you at first, that I should read such a passage of scripture on such an occasion; but it will not appear so long, when I inform you that my intention is, by opening and explaining the emblems of the cherubim, to lay before you the qualifications, duties, work, and usefulness of the ministers of the gospel" (Gill, *Collection of Sermons and Tracts*, 2:31).

example of Gill's ability as a biblical commentator and theologian.[63] Further, although a substantial amount of the sermon is spent determining the identity of the cherubim, Gill does not fail to apply his conclusions to pastoral work, arguing that pastors are to be "the instruments and means of quickening dead sinners, and of reviving and refreshing drooping saints."[64] Gill is particularly explicit about evangelistic responsibilities.[65] For example, from the placement of cherubim over the mercy seat in Heb 9:5, he concluded:

> And this, my Brother, is a principal part of your work, as one of the cherubs, to direct to Christ the mercy-seat, the channel of the grace and mercy of God to the souls of men; as God set forth Christ in his eternal purposes and decrees to be a propitiation . . . so you are to set him forth in your ministrations as the propitiation, propitiatory, and mercy-seat: let the mercy-seat be ever in view; keep in sight in all your ministrations the doctrine of atonement and satisfaction by the blood and sacrifice of Christ; let this be the polestar by which you steer the course of your ministry; direct souls to the throne of grace, to the mercy-seat, to God in Christ, where they may hope to find grace and mercy to help them in time of need.[66]

The other three published pastoral charges are more conventional in content, with Gill taking up texts from the Pastoral Epistles. From 1 Tim 4:16, Gill delivered a straightforward charge to George Braithwaite to take heed of himself, his doctrine,

---

[63] When identifying illusions to cherubim, and how this corresponds to ministers, Gill explicitly references passages from Genesis, Exodus, 1 Kings, 1 Chronicles, Ezra, Nehemiah, Psalms, Proverbs, Isaiah, Jeremiah, Ezekiel, Zechariah, Matthew, Luke, John, Acts, Romans, 1–2 Corinthians, Galatians, Ephesians, Philippians, 1 Thessalonians, 1–2 Timothy, Hebrews, 1 Peter, and, repeatedly, Revelation. He also deals with some negative systematic implications of interpreting the cherubim as divine persons and demonstrates his command of Jewish sources and commentators, regularly relying on the opinions of such scholars throughout the sermon.

[64] Gill, *Collection of Sermons and Tracts*, 2:39.

[65] For example, he asserts: "Now the cherubim were in this emblems of ministers of the gospel, the servants of the most high God; whose work it is to shew unto men the way of life and salvation by Jesus Christ. And this is the business that you, my Brother, should be constantly employed in … acquaint all that you are concerned with, that salvation is by Christ alone; that God has chosen and appointed him to be his salvation to the ends of the earth; and that he has appointed men to salvation alone by him; that he has sent him into the world to be the Saviour of them; this is the faithful saying, and worthy of all acceptation, you are to publish and proclaim, that Christ came into the world to save the chief of sinners; and that by his obedience, sufferings and death, he is become the author of eternal salvation to them; and that there is salvation in him, and in no other; and that there is no other name given under heaven among men whereby they can be saved. Souls sensible of sin and danger, and who are crying out, What shall we do to be saved? you are to observe, and point out Christ the tree of life unto them; and say, as some of the cherubs did to one in such circumstances, Believe on the Lord Jesus Christ, and thou shalt be saved, Acts 16:31" (Gill, *Collection of Sermons and Tracts*, 2:35–36).

[66] Gill, *Collection of Sermons and Tracts*, 2:37–38. This is a refrain that Spurgeon would often repeat, for he also seen the doctrine of the atonement to be a "guiding star" like that of "the pole star" (Spurgeon, *The Metropolitan Tabernacle Pulpit Sermons* [London: Passmore & Alabaster, 1872], 18:73).

and continuing to do so.⁶⁷ Under his second heading, contrary to any allusion of antinomianism, Gill argued that a preacher must "be careful that the doctrine he teaches be according to godliness; that it is not contrary to the moral perfections of God, or has a tendency to promote a loose and licentious life; but that it is agreeable to, and may be a means of increasing, both internal and external holiness."⁶⁸ In this way, Gill set up the promotion of godliness as a litmus test for all doctrine and concluded "whatever doctrines are subversive of true piety, or strike at the life and power of godliness, are to be rejected."⁶⁹ In Braithwaite's charge, Gill once again gravitated towards the evangelistic responsibilities of the pastor. He closed by reflecting on the twofold motivation given in 1 Tim 4:16, the salvation of both the minister and hearer, and concluded: "What can, or does, more strongly engage ministers to take heed to themselves, to their doctrine, and abide therein, than this? That they may be useful in the conversion, and so in the salvation of precious and immortal souls, which are of more worth than a world."⁷⁰

From 2 Tim 1:13, Gill delivered the threefold charge to John Reynolds to: be principally concerned about the form of sound words; hold it fast; and to do so in faith and love.⁷¹ Most of the sermon focuses on the first point, with Gill first asserting that scripture contains a certain form of sound words, being "a scheme and system of gospel-truths" which ministers ought not to deviate from or contradict, and then outlining a ten point summary of this system.⁷² These points supply a succinct summary of what Gill understood as the fundamental tenets of the Christian faith, being the doctrines of the Trinity; God's everlasting love for the elect; eternal, personal, and particular election; the covenant of grace; original sin; redemption by Christ; justification by Christ's imputed righteousness; pardon, peace and reconciliation by Christ's blood; regeneration, effectual calling, conversion and sanctification by the Spirit; and the final perseverance of the saints.⁷³ Given this charge likely came shortly after Reynolds had publicly recited his own ordinand's statement of faith, one can only hope that he remembered to adequately reference all ten of Gill's essential doctrines.⁷⁴

While the three sermons discussed above provide ample evidence of Gill's

---

⁶⁷ Gill, *Collection of Sermons and Tracts*, 2:2.

⁶⁸ Gill, *Collection of Sermons and Tracts*, 2:9.

⁶⁹ Gill, *Collection of Sermons and Tracts*, 2:9.

⁷⁰ Gill, *Collection of Sermons and Tracts*, 2:13.

⁷¹ Gill, *Collection of Sermons and Tracts*, 2:49.

⁷² Gill, *Collection of Sermons and Tracts*, 2:52–53.

⁷³ Gill, *Collection of Sermons and Tracts*, 2:53–62.

⁷⁴ The account of Reynolds' ordination given by Ivimey appears to follow the form of the standard ordination service described above: "On this occasion Dr. Gill delivered the introductory part of the service, and asked the usual questions from the church … Dr. Stennett offered up the ordination prayer. Dr. Gill gave the charge, from 2 Tim. i. 13; Mr. Burford prayed; Mr. B. Wallin preached to the people from 1 Cor. xii. 25; and Mr. Anderson closed the service by prayer" (Ivimey, *A History of the English Baptists*, 4:322).

ability as a commentator and theologian, it is his charge to his nephew that most comprehensively reveals his pastoral theology.[75] Preaching from 2 Tim 2:7, "Consider what I say, and the Lord give thee understanding in all things," Gill took the opportunity "to lay before you, the pastor of this church, for your consideration, various things relative to the work you have been chosen, and called unto, and the office you have been invested with."[76] Gill spends the majority of the charge urging his nephew to consider the great business and honorable work of ministry. In doing so, he identifies four parts of this work: ministration of the word; administration of gospel-ordinances; care of the discipline of the church; and visitation of the members of the church.[77] He also reflects on the qualifications necessary for the work, as well as some of the discouragements and encouragements that attend it. Gill's sermon contains many wise words that are still profitable for those undertaking this great work today. Further, he once again emphasizes the evangelistic responsibilities of the pastor, arguing that this should include personal visitation:

> Moreover, you will be called upon sometimes to visit sick persons, who are not members of the church; and who may be strangers to the grace of God, and the way of salvation by Christ; and who have been either profane persons, or resting upon their civility and morality, pleasing themselves, that they have wronged no man, and have done that which is right between man and man; and now in dying circumstances, hope, on this account, things will be well with them; and whose relatives may be afraid of your saying any thing to interrupt this carnal peace; yet, be faithful, labour to shew the one and the other their wretched and undone state by nature; the necessity of repentance towards God, and faith in our Lord Jesus Christ, in his blood, righteousness, and atoning sacrifice, for peace, pardon, justification, and salvation.[78]

---

[75] For this reason, the whole of this charge has been appended to this publication.

[76] Gill, *Collection of Sermons and Tracts*, 2:15.

[77] Gill, *Collection of Sermons and Tracts*, 2:16–22.

[78] Gill, *Collection of Sermons and Tracts*, 2:21–22. In a funeral sermon for John Davenport, one of his deacons, Gill suggests what such earnest evangelism should look like: "it is the business of a minister at such a time to shew the sick man what is right for him to do: if the sick man is stupid and insensible of his state and condition by nature; then he is to inform him that God made man upright, but he by sinning lost his uprightness; and this is not now to be found in men, but must be had in another: he is to labour to convince him of the sin of his nature, and the sinfulness of his life and actions; and to shew him the exceeding sinfulness of sin, and the just demerit of it, eternal death and damnation, and the absolute necessity of repentance for it. If the sick man is a sensible man, and is depressed under a sense of sin, and the guilt of it, and under fearful apprehensions of wrath and ruin; the minister is to set before him Christ, and him crucified; he is to tell him of his blood, righteousness and sacrifice, and the efficacy of them to take away sin; and to direct and encourage him to believe in Christ; assuring him, that whoever believes in him shall be saved. Add to this, if the sick man is a good man, a truly gracious man, and yet has doubts and fears of his uprightness, and the truth of grace in him; then, the minister observing that this is the fruit of unbelief, and of Satan's temptations, is to do all he can to clear up this point to him, that he is truly a regenerated and converted man; that he has truth in the inner part, and that the work of grace is begun, which will be performed in him: and this, as one rightly

John Gill on ordination
Other than the oddity of preaching from Ezekiel 10:20, Gill's ordination sermons are just as his hearers would have expected. Wheeler suggests the main purpose of the charge was to describe the motivations, character, qualifications, duties, and purposes of ministers of the gospel, which is exactly what Gill accomplishes in his sermons.[79] Further, the pastoral theology contained in them is consistent with that found in other Particular Baptist ordination sermons of the period, with themes such as the call of a church, the character and qualifications of a pastor, the means of improving ministerial gifts, church discipline, the purpose and content of preaching, the administration of the ordinances, and the importance of visitation generally prominent.[80] Additionally, the ordination services that Gill took part in appear to have typically followed the standard order outlined above. Nevertheless, despite the uniformity of Gill's pastoral theology and ordination services, his theology of ordination diverged in at least one key respect. Rather than accepting the ordination practices of his day uncritically, Gill came to conclusions that not only deviated from the previous pastors of his own church, but also the position of the wider Particular Baptist world, as set out in the Second London Confession.[81]

Gill was the first pastor of Horselydown to reject the imposition of hands for all baptized believers, believing this to be based on a Jewish practice that is fulfilled in Christ.[82] With respect to ordination, Gill generally agreed with the understanding of Particular Baptists outlined above, albeit he also wanted to stress emphases in the Savoy Declaration that were not explicit in the Second London Confession.[83] Nevertheless, Gill deviated from both documents by rejecting the imposition of

---

observes, is the hardest work that the ministers of the gospel have, to make men understand and see their own uprightness: all this being done, then he is gracious; the minister is gracious, has pity and compassion on the sick man, and speaks of the grace of God to him, and makes a gracious supplication for him; (so some render the words) and prays in the following manner; 'O Lord God, deliver this sick man from going down to the pit, redeem his life from destruction; for I find in the everlasting gospel, there is a ransom or atonement for sin provided for such persons'" (Gill, *Collection of Sermons and Tracts*, 1:516–17).

[79] Wheeler, "Eminent Spirituality and Eminent Usefulness," 110.

[80] Wheeler, "Eminent Spirituality and Eminent Usefulness;," 116–62. Gill's sermon published below covers every one of these themes.

[81] It remains to be seen whether other leading Particular Baptists prior to Gill made similar arguments or arrived at such conclusions. However, it is surely significant that such objections or objectors were not important enough to warrant the exclusion of the imposition of hands at ordination from the Second London Confession, which, for example, was the case with respect to the imposition of hands on believers more generally as a result of there being common disagreement over the practice.

[82] See, for example, his brief treatment of the topic in Gill, *Complete Body of Doctrinal and Practical Divinity*, 1:x.

[83] For example, considering the ordination of officers more generally, echoing the Savoy Declaration, Gill highlighted the "essence" of ordination was the election of the officer by the congregation and their acceptance of that call, and asserted that the public service was "no other than a declaration of that." As a result, he concluded, "Election and ordination are spoken of as the same; the latter is expressed and explained by the former" (Gill, *Complete Body of Doctrinal and Practical Divinity*, 2:580).

hands at ordination.[84] Gill believed the record of Paul and Barnabas appointing elders in Acts 14:23 was key in determining how pastors were to be appointed. From it he observed, "Though there was χειροτονια, a stretching out of the hands [that is in suffrage when the church selected them]; yet there was no χειροθεσια, imposition of hands, used at the ordination."[85] For Gill, the practice of imposition at ordination lacked clear scriptural support.

Gill rejected the interpretation of 1 Timothy 4:14 in the Second London Confession, on which it based the practice of imposing hands at ordination.[86] He believed the biblical text made clear that this was an exceptional event, as it resulted in Timothy receiving a special gift of the Holy Spirit. Therefore, he stated "since gifts have ceased being conveyed this way, the rite of laying on of hands in ordinations seems useless, and of no avail."[87] On this basis, Gill concluded that "the hands of ministers *being now empty*, and they having no gifts to convey through the use of this rite, of course it ought to cease, and should" (emphasis added).[88]

It is unclear whether Gill caused widespread change among Particular Baptists in his lifetime. While his views did not necessarily preclude him from participating in services with imposition, it is perhaps significant that it does not appear to have been practiced in at least several of the ordinations he took part in.[89] What is clear

---

[84] George suggests Gill regarded "the rite of ordination through the laying on of hands as a popish trifle which would be better left undone" (Timothy George, "The Ecclesiology of John Gill," in *Life and Thought of John Gill*, 233). However, while this was certainly the view of Spurgeon, as shown below, it is unclear that Gill was as strongly influenced by concerns over Roman Catholicism and apostolic succession. It is more likely that his related rejection of the imposition of hands on all believers, and the implication that this was connected to the giving of the Holy Spirit, was of greater concern to him.

[85] Gill, *Complete Body of Doctrinal and Practical Divinity*, 2:581.

[86] Article 9 of Chapter XXVI, see McGlothlin, *Baptist Confessions of Faith*, 266.

[87] John Gill, *An Exposition of the New Testament* (London: Mathews and Leigh, 1809), 3:298.

[88] Gill, *Complete Body of Doctrinal and Practical Divinity*, 2:583. Jan Abrahamse helpfully summarizes, "The core of Gill's objection toward ordination is the presumed meaninglessness of the visible and physical rite. Nothing happens and, importantly, nothing more needs to happen, for the candidate is already elected by the church" (Jan Martijn Abrahamse, *Ordained Ministry in Free Church Perspective* [Leiden: Brill, 2020], 51).

[89] For example, Ivimey points out that while John Noble was "much opposed to the practice of laying on of hands at the ordination of ministers," he was content to moderate his views in order to preach at John Gill's own ordination service, where imposition of hands took place (Ivimey, *History of the English Baptists*, 2:345).

While more comprehensive research would need to be carried out to confirm this, there is no mention of the imposition of hands in several records of John Reynolds' ordination, for whom Gill delivered the pastoral charge. See John Andrews Jones, *Bunhill Memorials: Sacred Reminiscences of Three Hundred Ministers and Other Persons of Note, who are Buried in Bunhill Fields, of Every Denomination ; with the Inscriptions on Their Tombs and Gravestones, and Other Historical Information Respecting Them, from Authentic Sources* (London: James Paul, 1848), 229. Walter Wilson, *The History and Antiquities of Dissenting Churches and Meeting Houses, in London, Westminster, and Southwark* (London: Walter Wilson, 1808), 2:581. Similarly, there is no reference to the laying on of hands in the records of the ordinations of George Braithwaite and John Davis. See Ivimey, *History of the English Baptists*, 4:228. Geoffrey F. Nuttall, "The Letter-Book of John Davis (1731–1795) of Waltham Abbey," *Baptist Quarterly* 24 (1971): 59.

is that he was able to bring about change in his own church.[90] After a decade of ministry, at a church meeting in 1729, Gill explained his objections to the practice of imposition.[91] Seemingly convinced, the congregation asked him to draw up a new confessional document, which was duly approved at their next meeting on March 25, 1729.[92] This document was much shorter than Keach's confession, and not only removed references to imposing hands on all believers, but also doing so at ordination.[93] As a result, under Gill, the church moved from having the imposition of hands on all believers as a term of communion, embedded within their confessional documents and being submitted to by all members, to no longer even practicing it at the ordination of its officers.

Ordination after John Gill

After his death in 1771, this initially remained the position of Gill's church. For example, his replacement, John Rippon, received no imposition of hands at his ordination.[94] Likewise, deacons appointed in 1774 and 1791 were "'invested'-- by 'the right hand of fellowship.'"[95] However, two decades after his death, Gill's influence was fading. Rippon did not share his predecessor's views, and contrary to his own church's practice, ordained pastors by imposition elsewhere during these years. A month after the ordinations of those deacons in 1791, Rippon brought his views before the church and narrowly persuaded them to return to imposing hands at ordination.[96] However, in Rippon's later years, this was practiced less frequently and the church never returned to laying hands on all believers as under Stinton, Keach, and Rider.[97]

Rippon's position reflects that of other leading Particular Baptists of his generation.[98] For example, when William Carey (1761-1834) was ordained in

[90] As explained below, this change did not happen immediately with respect to the laying on of hands on all believers. For example, Payne points out that two sisters, who had not previously had hands laid upon them, had to come under the ordinance upon transferring their membership to Gill's church in 1721 (Payne, "Baptists and the Laying on of Hands," 213).

[91] White, "John Gill in London," 87.

[92] Seymour J. Price, "Dr. John Gill's Confession of 1729," *Baptist Quarterly* 4 (1929): 367.

[93] Price, "Dr. John Gill's Confession of 1729," 369.

[94] Manley, *"Redeeming Love Proclaim,"* 38.

[95] Manley, *"Redeeming Love Proclaim,"* 54.

[96] This was perhaps prompted by the fact that prior to the ordinations in 1791, a member proposed they be conducted by imposition, only withdrawing this motion when realizing it would generate a "warm discussion" among other members. Gill's ongoing influence even two decades after his death is evident not only from this but from the fact that Rippon only narrowly won the later vote. While 30 members supported him, another 28 members voted against the change (Ernest A. Payne, "The Appointment of Deacons: Notes from the Southwark Minute Book, 1719-1802," *Baptist Quarterly* 17 [1957]: 90-91).

[97] Manley, *"Redeeming Love Proclaim,"* 55.

[98] For example, on February 28, 1798, Rippon offered the ordination prayer and, along with Abraham Booth and others, laid hands on an ordinand of the church at Somers Town in London. See Ivimey, *History*

1791, John Ryland, Jr. (1753–1825) prayed with imposition of hands, and John Sutcliff (1752–1814), Samuel Pearce (1766–1799), and Andrew Fuller all took part.[99] Further, some of the statements made by these men regarding the role of visiting ministers is in direct contrast with Gill's theological understanding of ordination.[100] Regardless, the imposition of hands remained a central part of ordination from the fact it was often defended during services.[101] For this reason, G. Hugh Wamble concludes that Particular Baptists did not follow Gill in rejecting imposition.[102]

However, despite this, there are signs that Gill's opposition and arguments started a slow changing of the tide. While Rippon's *Baptist Annual Register* throughout the 1790s shows that ordination services followed the same pattern as before, imposition is mentioned in as many cases as it is not, with several references to "the right hand of fellowship" and at least one stated to "have been *without* imposition of hands."[103] Further, when Sutcliff defends the practice at Thomas Morgan's ordination, he acknowledges that some in attendance disapprove of it.[104] He even echoes the language and acknowledges the argument of Gill by admitting, "Not that by this we can convey any extraordinary gifts, or additional qualifications to the person ordained ... No; *Our hands are empty*" (emphasis added).[105]

As the nineteenth century continued, it became even clearer the practice "was

---

of the English Baptists, 4:409.

[99] George Smith, *The Life of William Carey* (London: John Murray, 1885), 49–50. For further examples, see Wheeler, "Eminent Spirituality and Eminent Usefulness," 93, n.86.

[100] Ryland, Fuller, and Sutcliff likewise all partook in the ordination of Thomas Morgan (1776–1857) in 1802, which also included the imposition of hands. During his introductory discourse, Sutcliff asserted that it was "natural to infer" that such ordination belonged to men already in office, and so while the people of the church choose, elders from other churches are to ordain (John Ryland, Andrew Fuller, and John Sutcliff, *The Difficulties of the Christian Ministry, and the Means of surmounting them; with the Obedience of Churches to their Pastors Explained and Enforced* [Birmingham: J. Belcher, 1802], 6). Such language stands in contrast to Gill's insistence that ordination is nothing other than election by the congregation, and that the involvement of other ministers is but the recognition of that choice for the satisfaction of those churches in communion with them, with ministers only assisting, whether by prayer or word of exhortation, if that is desired (Gill, *Complete Body of Doctrinal and Practical Divinity*, 2:580). Fuller held an intermediate view, explaining he "considered the imposition of hands by neighbouring ministers as keeping with the New Testament order and example, but that the nature of ordination was founded in the free choice of the church itself; the imposition of hands was proper and orderly, but not essential" (Keith S. Grant, *Andrew Fuller and the Evangelical Renewal of Pastoral Theology* [Eugene, OR: Wipf and Stock, 2013], 71).

[101] Wheeler, "Eminent Spirituality and Eminent Usefulness," 98, n.104–106. For example, reflecting on 1 Tim 5:22 during an introductory discourse at Thomas Morgan's ordination, Sutcliff reasons Paul would not have "expressed the business of Ordination" by the phrase "if he had not considered the laying on of hands as essential unto it" (Ryland, Fuller, and Sutcliff, *Difficulties of the Christian Ministry*, 8).

[102] Wamble, "Baptist Ordination practices to 1845," 19.

[103] Geoffrey F. Nuttall, "The Baptist Churches and Their Ministers in the 1790s," *Baptist Quarterly* 30 (1984): 385.

[104] Ryland, Fuller, and Sutcliff, *Difficulties of the Christian Ministry*, 8.

[105] Ryland, Fuller, and Sutcliff, *Difficulties of the Christian Ministry*, 7.

no longer uncontested."¹⁰⁶ A key reason for this was the stand taken by Spurgeon, Gill's eventual successor. After being called in 1854, he informed the church that he not only objected to the imposition of hands, but also to there even being an ordination service.¹⁰⁷ As a result, he became pastor without either. Later explaining this, he asked, "Whence comes the whole paraphernalia of ordination as observed among some Dissenters? Since there is no special gift to bestow, why in any case the laying on of *empty hands*?" (emphasis added).¹⁰⁸ Ernst A. Payne argues such statements from Spurgeon, alongside rising anti-clericalism, were key in explaining why imposition "appears to have fallen into disuse" by the late nineteenth century.¹⁰⁹ Reflecting on continued apathy to the practice in the twentieth century, Jan Abrahamse observes Spurgeon's "words have not lost their influence over the years."¹¹⁰ However, as this article has shown, this is equally true for Gill, whom Spurgeon appears to echo. For this reason, these two men were not only united by the remarkably similar circumstances of their lives, but also by their call for the laying aside of empty hands.

---

[106] Abrahamse, *Ordained Ministry in Free Church Perspective*, 52.

[107] Spurgeon, *C.H. Spurgeon's Autobiography*, 1:356. The position of Spurgeon on ordination, and the imposition of hands in particular, is well outlined and assessed by Abrahamse. See Jan Martijn Abrahamse, "Charles Spurgeon and the Curious Case of the 'Empty Hands': The Rise of Anti-Sacramentalism among English Evangelicals" (paper presented at the Christianity and History Forum, All Nations Christian College, Ware, Hertfordshire, April 2017).

[108] C.H. Spurgeon, *The Sword and Trowel, 1874* (London: Passmore & Alabaster, 1874), 89.

[109] Payne, "Baptists and the Laying on of Hands," 206. Payne demonstrates that even when the use of ordination services increased again among Baptists in the twentieth century, imposition was simply considered to be an option alongside that of giving "the right hand of fellowship."

[110] Abrahamse, *Ordained Ministry in Free Church Perspective*, 52.

"Nursing fathers and … nursing mothers to the Israel of God": Benjamin Beddome on praying for godly rulers

Michael A.G. Haykin

Michael A.G. Haykin is Professor of Church History and Director, The Andrew Fuller Center for Baptist Studies at The Southern Baptist Theological Seminary, Louisville, KY.

Catechisms were central to the British and Irish Particular Baptist movement from its inception in the 1630s.[1] The most widely-used catechism in this community of Baptists was one commissioned by a national meeting of the denomination in June of 1693. A London pastor by the name of William Collins (d. 1702) was asked to draw it up, though many would later know it as *Keach's Catechism*, so-called after the prolific Baptist author Benjamin Keach (1640–1704).[2] Formally it was called *The Baptist Catechism* and was essentially a Baptist revision of the Presbyterian *Shorter Catechism* (1648).[3] By 1747, there had been no less than fifteen editions of this catechism.[4]

The usage of this catechism by Benjamin Beddome (1718–1795), whose pastoral ministry at Bourton-on-the-Water in the Cotswolds stretched from 1740 until his

---

[1] For the importance placed on catechetical literature by the early Nonconformist tradition, see Richard L. Greaves, "Introduction," in John Bunyan, *Instruction for the Ignorant, Light for Them that Sit in Darkness, Saved by Grace, Come, & Welcome, to Jesus Christ*, ed. Richard L. Greaves (Oxford: Clarendon, 1979), xxxiii–xliii.

[2] Joseph Ivimey, *A History of the English Baptists* (London, 1811), 1:533; idem, *A History of the English Baptists* (London, 1814), 2:397. J. Barry Vaughn, "Benjamin Keach," in *Baptist Theologians*, ed. Timothy George and David S. Dockery (Nashville, TN: Boardman Press, 1990), 66.

[3] For a reprint of this catechism, see *The Baptist Catechism*, ed. Paul King Jewett (Grand Rapids, MI: Baker, 1952).

[4] See, for example, *The Baptist-Catechism: or A Brief Instruction in the Principles of the Christian Religion*, 15th ed. (London: A. Ward, 1747).

death, can be taken as typical of the Baptist leadership of this era.[5] Beddome was thoroughly convinced that vital Christianity is a matter of both heart and head. He found the use of a catechism helpful in matching head knowledge to heart-felt faith.

During the early years of his ministry, Beddome used *The Baptist Catechism* widely. But he came to believe that the questions and answers of the catechism needed to be supplemented by further material. So, he composed what was printed in 1752 as *A Scriptural Exposition of the Baptist Catechism by Way of Question and Answer*.[6] It basically reproduced the wording and substance of *Keach's Catechism* but added various sub-questions and answers to each of the main questions. The *Scriptural Exposition* proved to be fairly popular. There were two editions during Beddome's lifetime, the second of which was widely used at the Bristol Baptist Academy, the sole British Baptist seminary for much of the eighteenth century. In the nineteenth century it was reprinted once in the British Isles and twice in the United States, the last printing being in 1849. John Rippon (1751–1836), who wrote the earliest biography of Beddome, rightly described it as "a compendium of Divinity."[7]

Now, in the section dealing with the second petition of the Lord's prayer—"Thy kingdom come"—Beddome added a substantial amount to the simple question in *Keach's Catechism*, "What do we pray for in the second petition?"[8] For instance, he asked the following questions under this heading and answered them as below:

Should we pray for the farther calling of the Gentiles? Yes. *That thy way may be known upon earth, and thy saving health among all nations*, Psalm 67:2. And for the conversion of the Jews? Yes. *My heart's desire and prayer to God for Israel is, that they may be saved*, Romans 10:1 Should we pray that magistrates might be raised up to favour the gospel? Yes. That *Kings* might *be nursing fathers and*

---

[5] The earliest biographical account of Beddome's life is an extensive obituary written by John Rippon (1751–1836), "Rev. Benjamin Beddome, A.M. Bourton-on-the-Water, Gloucesteshire," *Baptist Annual Register* 2 (1794–1797): 314–326. This account was largely reproduced by Joseph Ivimey in *A History of the English Baptists* (London: Isaac Taylor Hinton; Holdsworth & Ball, 1830), 4:461–469. Two significant biographical studies that appeared in the course of the nineteenth century are the "Memoir" attached to *Sermons Printed from the Manuscripts of the late Rev. Benjamin Beddome* (London: William Ball, 1835), ix–xxviii, and the lengthy account of Beddome's ministry in Thomas Brooks, *Pictures of the Past: The History of the Baptist Church, Bourton-on-the-Water* (London: Judd & Glass, 1861), 21–66. For more recent studies, see Michael A.G. Haykin, with Roy M. Paul and Jeongmo Yoo, ed., *Glory to the Three Eternal: Tercentennial Essays on the Life and Writings of Benjamin Beddome (1718–1795)*, Monographs in Baptist History, vol. 13 (Eugene, OR: Pickwick, 2019).

[6] Benjamin Beddome, *A Scriptural Exposition of the Baptist Catechism by Way of Question and Answer*, 2nd ed. (Bristol: W. Pine, 1776). For a digital version, see https://baptistcatechism.org/beddome/ (accessed April 27, 2023).

[7] John Rippon, "Rev. Benjamin Beddome, A.M. Bourton-on-the-Water, Gloucestershire," *Baptist Annual Register* 2 (1794–1797): 322

[8] For the original question and answer, see *The Baptist-Catechism*, 15th ed., 45. It is Question 109.

Queens nursing mothers to the Israel of God, Isaiah 49:23 And that ministers might be raised up to preach the gospel? Yes. *Pray ye the Lord of the harvest that he will send forth labourers into his harvest*, Matthew 11:38. And that the gospel, wherever it is preached, might be followed with success? Yes. *That the word of the Lord might have free course, and be glorified* 2 Thessalonians 3:1.[9]

To pray the second petition of the Lord's Prayer, "Thy kingdom," necessarily entailed for this Cotswolds pastor prayer for the conversion of Gentiles around the world along with that of the Jewish people as well as prayer for the raising up of gospel preachers and divine blessing on their preaching of the Word of God. Embedded in the heart of this prayer for the evangelistic extension of God's rule is the encouragement to pray for "Kings [to] … be nursing fathers and Queens nursing mothers to the Israel of God."[10] Beddome based this particular exhortation upon Isa 49:23. In other words, Christians were to pray that secular rulers might be converted and help facilitate the spread of the gospel.

What did rule by these Christian monarchs look like in Beddome's mind? This specific passage does not elaborate. His contemporary, John Gill (1697–1771), though, used the very same text in his commentary on Isaiah—which appeared in 1757, five years after Beddome's comment—to argue that such rulers will "show favour and respect to the church and people of God, grant them liberty, and protect and defend them in their religious privileges" (Isa 49:23). Gill identified some in the past who had fulfilled this role: in the Persian Empire there was Cyrus (c.600–530 BC), Ahasuerus and Esther, and in late Antiquity, Constantine (c.272–337), his mother Helena (c.246/8–c.330), and Theodosius the Great (347–395). But, according to Gill, this text would have "a far greater accomplishment in the latter-day glory," a term that had originated in the Puritan era to designate a future era of millennial blessings.[11] Gill was convinced that there was coming a time of remarkable world-wide blessing for the church, and Christian rulers would play a key role in this period of time.

Gill further elaborated in his *A Body of Practical Divinity* (1770), which Gill's son-in-law published in the year before Gill's death. Gill noted that this millennial era was to be a period of history when "all kings shall fall down before Christ; when kings shall come to the brightness of Zion, or to the church's rising, and when her gates shall stand open continually for kings to enter in, and become church-members; and when kings shall be nursing-fathers, and queens nursing-

---

[9] Beddome, *Scriptural Exposition of the Baptist Catechism*, 181. The biblical references have been modernized.

[10] Beddome, *Scriptural Exposition of the Baptist Catechism*, 181.

[11] John Gill, *An Exposition of the Books of the Prophets of the Old Testament* (London: G. Keith, 1757), 1:273. In his *A Body of Practical Divinity; or, A system of Practical Truths, deduced from the Sacred Scriptures* (London: George Keith, 1770), Gill reckoned that "Constantine, the first Christian emperor, [was] thought to be a very good man" (Gill, *Body of Practical Divinity*, 451).

mothers."[12] Now, what is fascinating is that Gill believed evidently that it was not only in this future era of the "latter-day glory" that Christian monarchs were to be such a blessing to the church. Gill was conscious that what applied to the theocratic government of ancient Israel was not to be expected in the constitutional monarchy of Great Britain, and yet he argued:

> Our kings have a concern in the making of laws; that is, they have a negative voice, and can put a check upon any laws, and refuse to sign them made by the other branches of the legislature; and it is their duty to refuse to sign such laws as are not salutary to their subjects, or are contrary to the laws of God, and to the fundamental laws of the state. … Christian kings have a peculiar concern with the laws of the two tables, that they are observed, and the violaters of them punished; as sins against the first table, idolatry, worshipping of more gods than one, and of graven images, blaspheming the name of God, perjury, and false-swearing, and profanation of the day of worship: and those against the second table; as disobedience to parents, murder, adultery, theft, bearing false witness, etc. most of which, under the former former dispensation, were capital crimes, and punishable with death; and tho' the punishment of them, at least not all of them, may not be inflicted with that rigor now as then; yet they are punishable in some way or another; which it is the duty of magistrates to take care of.[13]

It is fascinating to find Gill affirming here what a significant number of his fellow Particular Baptists in the long eighteenth century would have completely rejected, namely, the state's role in the enforcement of the first table of the law. Indeed, the above quotation seems to better fit with the heyday of the Puritan era of the previous century.

But what of Beddome? Would he have agreed with Gill's understanding of the exact duties of the ruler in this present age? However one answers this latter question—and at this stage of my research into Beddome, I have no clear answer—I think it is evident from the above quotation from Gill that Beddome's exhortation from Isaiah 49:23 to pray for goldy rulers would certainly have received an amen from Gill.[14] In sum, one aspect of our praying for God's kingdom to be manifest in this world, according to these two Baptist divines of the long eighteenth century is that God might raise up godly rulers, "nursing fathers and … nursing mothers to the Israel of God."

---

[12] Gill, *Body of Practical Divinity*, 452.

[13] Gill, *Body of Practical Divinity*, 452–453.

[14] By the way, it is also interesting that Beddome, who had a considerable library, does not appear to have possessed any title from Gill's voluminous pen. Gill does not appear to have exercised a significant influence on the Cotswolds divine.

William Carey (1761–1834) and his books[1]

Austin Walker

Austin Walker is the retired pastor of Maidenbower Baptist Church, Crawley, Surrey. He is currently a member of Castlefields Church, Derby, and an occasional preacher. He is the author of The Excellent Benjamin Keach *(2nd ed., 2015), the definitive biography of the seventeenth-century Baptist leader.*

Writing to John Ryland, Jr. (1753–1825) towards the end of 1811, William Carey told his long-standing friend: "I am ... more in my element in the translation of the word of God than in any other employment, and now begin to entertain an idea that I may yet live to see this work, compleated in most of the languages in which it has begun."[2] By this time Carey had been working in India for eighteen years.

The translation of the Bible into the many languages of the Indian sub-continent and even further afield became Carey's lifelong priority. Early in 1793 before he left for India, he had met William Ward (1769–1823) for the first time at John Rippon's (1751–1836) church in London. Ward was from Derby and a printer by trade. He happened to be in London visiting friends. Carey seized the opportunity to unfold to him the desire and purpose of his heart respecting biblical translations. As they parted, he laid his hand on Ward's shoulder and said, "I hope, by God's blessing, to have the Bible translated and ready for the press in four or five years. You must come and print it for us."[3] Ward joined him in 1799 together with Joshua Marshman (1768–1837). Carey, Ward, and Marshman were to become the well-known "Serampore Trio."

When he sailed for Bengal with his family and with Dr. John Thomas (1757–1800) on the *Krön Princessa Maria* in June 1793, the same priority dictated how he spent his time. He used much of that five-month voyage learning Bengali from his missionary colleague. Combining his own knowledge of Hebrew with Thomas'

[1] This article was first presented as an Evangelical Library Annual Lecture on Monday June 6, 2011.

[2] William Carey, Letter to Ryland, December 10, 1811, in *The Journal and Selected Letters of William Carey*, ed. Terry G. Carter (Macon, GA: Smith and Helwys, 2000), 161.

[3] S. Pearce Carey, *William Carey D.D., Fellow of Linnaean Society* (London: Hodder and Stoughton, [1926]), 119.

knowledge of Bengali, they began to work on the translation of Genesis. Some five years later in 1798 in a letter to his sister Ann Hobson (1763–1843) the same priority is reflected,

> The principal thing we see is the translation of the Bible into the Bengal language. This is now in considerable forwardness, and I expect will be finished in the next year, if God continues Health, and other requisite abilities: nor do I think that we are entirely without Seals to our Ministry, tho it is a difficult thing to say anything confidently.[4]

Carey was being somewhat optimistic however, as the New Testament was not completed until 1801 and the Old Testament not until 1809. Once completed, Carey did not rest satisfied. He was constantly revising his translations. The fifth revision of the Bengali Old Testament and the eighth revision of the New Testament were completed in 1832. Two years later, Carey, now over 70 years of age, lay dying. In his stronger moments he was still reading the proofs of the eighth edition of the New Testament.

William Carey's translation work was a remarkable achievement. The Bengali Bible was only the beginning. When Marshman died in 1837, Carey and his friends had translated the Bible into some 40 languages and dialects. Carey himself was responsible for translating the entire Bible into Bengali, Odia, Marathi, Hindi, Assamese, and Sanskrit, as well as portions of it into twenty-nine other tongues. Timothy George in his biography of Carey believes that such labours place the one-time obscure and poor cobbler from Northamptonshire among "the front ranks of Bible translators in Christian history alongside Jerome (c.342/7–420), [John] Wycliffe [c.1328–1384], [Martin] Luther [1483–1546], [William] Tyndale [c.1494–c.1536] and Erasmus [1466–1536]."[5]

The purpose of this article is very selective in that it considers Carey and his books. Many biographies and books have already been written about Carey so I shall assume at least a general knowledge of his life and work and his remarkable perseverance despite the many setbacks he faced. We shall firstly, consider the books besides the Bible translations that Carey produced in connection with that work; secondly, show what he believed about "the Book"--the Bible--and why it's translation into many languages became his life-long priority; and then thirdly, see which books in addition to the Bible helped to shape his theology, mission practice and translation priorities and what led him in 1792 to produce his most famous book, *An Enquiry into the Obligation of Christians to Use Means for the Conversion of the Heathens.*

---

[4] Timothy D. Whelan, ed., *Baptist Autographs in the John Rylands Library of Manchester, 1741–1845* (Macon, GA: Mercer University Press, 2009), 90.

[5] Timothy George, *Faithful Witness: The Life and Mission of William Carey* (Leicester: Inter-Varsity, 1991), 141.

Some of the books Carey produced besides his translations of the Bible
While Carey was translating the Bible into Bengali, he became increasingly aware that Bengali often used Sanskrit expressions. That provided him with a challenge. He rose to it with typical Carey-like determination and set himself the task of mastering Sanskrit as well. He recognised that learned Brahmins looked down on any other language besides Sanskrit. If his ministry was to have any lasting impact on India, then he was persuaded that he had to tackle learning the sacred language of ancient Hindu civilisation. By 1808 he had produced the Sanskrit New Testament, followed ten years later by the Old Testament. Carey's aim was to give to the cultured hierarchy the "true Shastras" in place of the false ones. Instead of the Hindu Vedas and Upanishads, dominated by their myths of transmigration and pseudo-incarnations, Carey gave them the Bible with its true account of God's redeeming love in his incarnate Son, the Lord Jesus Christ and the regenerating power of the Spirit of God.

However, Carey's work of translating the Bible into Sanskrit led him to compile a dictionary and a grammar. Such books did not exist before Carey produced them and they were to become the basis for the modern critical study of this ancient classical language. Not everyone in England approved of his other ventures, the translation into Bengali from Sanskrit of the traditional Hindu epics––long poems celebrating the deeds of legendary heroes––like the *Ramayana*. They thought he was wasting his time, including his closest friend and loyal supporter Andrew Fuller (1754–1815). Carey, in typical thorough fashion, had thought and prayed carefully about these undertakings. He had at least three reasons for doing so. Firstly, he argued, to counter the arguments of the Brahmins he needed to know their sacred writings. Secondly, it improved his knowledge of Sanskrit, thus enabling him to better translate the Bible. Thirdly, Carey was a practical man concerned to provide as much financial backing as possible for the publication of Christian literature and especially the scriptures. Since there was an interest and demand for such Hindu texts, he was prepared to use the profits of this scheme to provide more revenue for the Serampore Press and the spread of the gospel.

In 1800 his first colleague in the work in India, John Thomas died. Shortly before Thomas' death, William Carey had been appointed a tutor in Bengali at the Fort William College in Calcutta. He, together with his colleagues, Ward and Marshman, had considered very carefully whether this was a wise move or whether it would prove to be a distraction to the work of the mission. According to Marshman, "we laid our heads together with the gravity of a conclave of Cardinals."[6] The college was founded to provide advanced training for the sons of the East India Company officials, the civil servants of the next generation. Carey taught there from 1801 until 1830 and became a tutor not only in Bengali but also Sanskrit and Marathi.

Carey's work in the college was a handmaid to his work of translation. He produced dictionaries in three languages––Bengali, Sanskrit, and Marathi––and

---

[6] As quoted in George, *Faithful Witness*, 145–146.

grammars in seven different languages.⁷ He explained to Ryland, "The necessity which lies upon me, of acquiring so many languages, obliges me to study and write out the grammar of each of them, and to attend closely to all their irregularities, and peculiarities."⁸ He was able to have around him some of the most learned native pundits, or expert scholars, to help him master the Indian languages and their particular dialects. Carey effectively became a senior research professor with a team of able scholars who helped him in his translation work.⁹

There were other advantages too. Carey's salary from the college became the primary means of financial support for the Serampore ministry although there was also income derived from the Marshmans' boarding school and revenue from their educational publications. Furthermore, because Carey was in Calcutta from Tuesday to Thursday, he used his evenings once college duties were over to preach the gospel to the poor and outcasts in the slums. By 1803, there was a place of worship in Calcutta with preaching in English twice on Sundays and Thursday evenings and in Bengali on Wednesday evenings.

In addition to the grammars and dictionaries Carey also provided prose books in Bengali for his students to read and also for children in the mission's elementary schools. Together with his son Felix (1786–1822) and some of the pundits, they produced some sixty books in prose, such as short stories, fables, essays, a version of John Bunyan's (1628–1688) *Pilgrim's Progress*, Indian history, a chemistry book, as well as the translations of the Sanskrit classics.¹⁰

Carey and Ward were also accustomed to writing Bengali tracts intended to be read out by anyone who could read. In 1802 Carey estimated their number, "perhaps not less than 20,000."¹¹ These he told his sisters have been "means of shaking the false faith of some, exciting very alarming fears in others, and we trust producing genuine conviction for sin in a few."¹² Writing to his brother, Carey mentions that he was also writing "a theological work in the Bengali language designed to show that the Hindus are going in a wrong Way, or rather that a renovation is necessary in their Disposition, Custom, and Sacred Writings."¹³ He added that it was occupying so much of his time that he was up until nearly midnight trying to complete it. Aware of the large European presence, especially English, in Calcutta, Carey was also responsible for producing tracts in English and other languages. He

---

⁷ Brian Stanley, *The History of the BMS, 1792–1992* (Edinburgh: T&T Clark, 1992), 51. Stanley notes also that these would have been signal achievements for someone with formal linguistic training. He judged them "extraordinary" for someone who completed his formal education at the age of twelve.

⁸ William Carey, Letter to John Ryland, December 10, 1811 in *Letters of William Carey*, ed. Carter, 162.

⁹ George, *Faithful Witness*, 146.

¹⁰ John Appleby, *I can plod: William Carey and the early years of the First Baptist Missionary Society* (London: Grace Publications Trust, 2007), 206.

¹¹ William Carey, Letter to John Ryland, December 10, 1811 in *Letters of William Carey*, ed. Carter, 157.

¹² William Carey, Letter to John Ryland, December 10, 1811 in *Letters of William Carey*, ed. Carter, 158.

¹³ William Carey, Letter to John Ryland, December 10, 1811 in *Letters of William Carey*, ed. Carter, 156.

wrote some of these but also published existing sermons like Philip Doddridge's (1702–1751) *Care of the Soul*.[14] This was published principally to address the careless and the Deists among his own countrymen.

It is evident that William Carey was not a man who ever let the grass grow under his feet. In 1818, there was a further major development, as he founded the Serampore College. The purpose of this institution was to provide theological education for Christian students. Carey's vision was such that he also included liberal arts studies in the curriculum. It was an interdenominational college, but all teachers were required to subscribe to essential evangelical doctrines such as the deity of Christ and penal substitutionary atonement. In addition to his work at Fort William College, Carey now became professor of divinity and a lecturer in botany and zoology. Without examining the latter subject, it is significant to notice that Carey developed magnificent gardens around the home of the "Serampore Trio" and the Serampore College. It was Carey who drew up the syllabus and prepared teaching materials for his lectures. He also published the first books on science and natural history in India.

For over forty years, from 1793 to 1834, William Carey laboured in India. He never returned to England unlike some of his colleagues. It is not possible to describe all that he accomplished during those years. It was remarkable by any standards. The testimonies of the men who knew him best tell us that he was a man marked by unwearied devotedness to his Lord and Saviour, by profound humility and self-denial. Eustace Carey (1791–1855), who observed him in India, said of his uncle, "the leading characteristics of Dr. Carey were his decision, his patient, persevering constancy, and his simplicity. A more decisive character, as to the main objects to which his life was consecrated, the page of history has seldom recorded."[15] He goes on to say that even as a boy, "at school … he never failed to master whatever came before him … he was always in earnest, was persevering, and adventurous" in whatever he did.[16]

We have to ask ourselves why was he so single-minded? Why did this man in his early thirties spend over forty years living and labouring in Bengal and devote so much time and energy to translation work? What were his motives? What were his convictions? What were the sources and reasons for those motives and convictions? Some of the answers to these questions now form the rest of this article.

What William Carey believed about "the Book"
In 1805, Carey and his Serampore colleagues drew up a "Form of Agreement" in which they stated the principles on which they thought it was their duty to act. This agreement was to be read publicly, at every mission station, at the three annual

---

[14] William Carey, Letter to John Ryland, December 10, 1811 in *Letters of William Carey*, ed. Carter, 1 157.

[15] Eustace Carey, *Memoir of William Carey, D.D., Late Missionary to Bengal; Professor of Oriental Languages in the College of Fort William, Calcutta* (London: Jackson and Walford, 1836), 616.

[16] Carey, *Memoir of William Carey*, 616.

meetings on the first Sunday of January, May, and October.[17] Section nine states:

> It becomes us also to labour with all our might in forwarding translations of the sacred scriptures in the languages of Hindoostan. The help which God has afforded us already is this work is a loud call to us to "go forward". So far, therefore, as God has qualified us to learn those languages which are necessary, we consider it our bounden duty to apply ourselves with unwearied assiduity in acquiring them. We consider the publication of the Divine Word throughout India as an object which we ought never to give up till accomplished, looking to the Fountain of all knowledge and strength to qualify us for this great work, and to carry us through it to the praise of His Holy Name.
>
> It becomes to us to use all assiduity in explaining and distributing the Divine Word on all occasions, and by every means in our power to excite the attention and the reverence of the natives towards it, as the fountain of eternal truth and the Message of Salvation to men. It is our duty to distribute, as extensively as possible, the different religious tracts which are published. Considering how much the general diffusion of the knowledge of Christ depends upon a liberal and constant distribution of the Word, and of these tracts, all over the country, we should keep this continually in mind, and watch all opportunities of putting even single tracts into the hands of those persons with whom we occasionally meet. We should endeavour to ascertain where large assemblies of the natives are to be found, that we may attend upon them, and gladden whole villages at once with the tidings of salvation.[18]

Such a statement indicates that Carey believed the Bible to be the Word of God. Timothy George argues that Carey was persuaded that "the Bible was the very Word of God, uniquely inspired by the Holy Spirit; a totally truthful revelation from God; an infallible authority for doctrine, ethics, and all matters pertaining to the Christian life."[19] Later on, he states that in his role as a translator, publisher, and distributor of the Bible and as a preacher of the gospel, William Carey was faithful to the Reformation principle of *sola Scriptura*.[20]

How did such a conviction work out in practice? With great care and much prayer Carey and his friends distributed translated versions of the New Testament. For example, tracts and one copy of the Bengali New Testament were distributed in a village near Calcutta. The villagers were told that the copy of the Bible should be given to the person who could read best. After three years some came from the

---

[17] A copy of the "Form of Agreement" is to be found in Aalbertinus Herman Oussoren, *William Carey, especially his Missionary Principles* (Leiden: A.W. Sijthoffs Uitgeversmaatsschappij., 1945), 274–284; Michael A.G. Haykin, *The Missionary Fellowship of William Carey* (Orlando, FL: Reformation Trust, 2018), 137–154.

[18] Haykin, *Missionary Fellowship of William Carey*, 150–151.

[19] George, *Faithful Witness*, 137.

[20] George, *Faithful Witness*, 173.

village to Carey asking how they could obtain the fruits from the death of Christ. Having read the Scriptures, they had been convicted of the sin of idolatry and come to trust in Christ for salvation. The reading of the Word and the powerful working of the Spirit of God led to their conversion. In similar fashion, by unaided study of the scriptures, five Kulin Brahmins, who were of the highest level of upper caste, were converted in 1812. Tom Nettles observes that "it is a significant insight into Carey's theology to realize that he and his compatriots expected that Scripture alone, under the blessing of the Spirit, would accomplish these things."[21]

In 1783, as a twenty three year old, Carey was baptised as a believer in the river Nene at Northampton, since he was convinced that believer's baptism was scriptural by reading his Bible.[22] While he was in his first pastorate in Moulton, Carey began to see from the same book the gradual unfolding of God's redeeming purposes in the Old Testament, especially the latter parts of Isaiah, and the New Testament. Those purposes continued to burn in his bones whatever John Ryland, Sr. (1723–1792) actually said to him at one particular Northamptonshire Baptist Association meeting.[23] Ryland was hostile to Carey's suggestion that they should consider "whether the command given to the apostles to teach all nations was not binding on all succeeding ministers to the end of the world, seeing that the accompanying promise was of equal extent."[24] In fact, Ryland had been influenced by high Calvinism, taught by men like John Brine (1703–1765). That biblical command became the cornerstone of Carey argument in *Enquiry*. Carey firmly rejected high Calvinism because he was persuaded it lacked biblical warrant, contradicting the mandate of Christ in Matt 28:19–20. Rather, Carey considered this mandate to be "the direct words of Jesus and thus a binding revelation upon the present generation as well as those under the 'immediate inspirations of the Holy Ghost.'"[25]

Thus, Carey believed firmly in the final authority of the Scriptures and in the sovereignty of Christ, that he had been given all authority and power, that he will conquer all nations, and that he uses means for bringing the nations to the obedience of faith. It was what the Word of God said, what Christ had commanded, that not only informed Carey but persuaded him, motivated him, and led him to "labour with all our might in forwarding translations of the sacred scriptures in the languages of Hindoostan."[26] For Carey it was nothing less than his "bounden duty."

---

[21] Tom Nettles, *The Baptists, Key People Involved in Forming a Baptist Identity, Vol. 1 Beginnings in Britain*, (Fearn, Ross-shire: Christian Focus, 2005), 298.

[22] Carey, *William Carey*, 38.

[23] The precise words and the actual date of the meeting are a matter of some dispute. The best discussion of the issues is to be found in Michael A.G. Haykin, *One Heart and One Soul: John Sutcliff of Olney, his friends and his times* (Darlington: Evangelical Press, 1994), 193–196.

[24] Carey, *William Carey*, 50.

[25] Nettles, *Baptists, Key People Involved in Forming a Baptist Identity*, 294.

[26] Haykin, *Missionary Fellowship of William Carey*, 150

Some of the books that shaped Carey's theology, mission principles, and translation priorities

When William Carey sailed for India in 1793, he went on behalf of the Particular Baptist Society for Propagating the Gospel among the Heathen (BMS). This society had only been formed the previous year in Kettering. John Ryland Jr., Reynold Hogg (1752–1843), William Carey, John Sutcliff (1752–1814), and Andrew Fuller formed the committee entrusted with the responsibilities of fulfilling the goals of the society. Carey had been a Particular Baptist pastor first at Moulton (1787–1789) and then at Leicester (1789–1793).[27] The church in Moulton however had General Baptist roots but had fallen into decline when Carey began to minister there. Nevertheless, they were happy to receive his ministry. By 1787, Carey had already embraced Calvinistic convictions as we shall see in due course.

He begun preaching in Hackleton Baptist Church in 1781 where he also met and then married Dorothy Plackett (1756–1807). However, he also began to preach every other week in Earls Barton, an arrangement that lasted for several years. Earls Barton was not far from Northampton, but the congregation had not formed themselves into a regular church. In 1782 he first met Fuller and Sutcliff and heard Fuller preach at the annual assembly of the Northamptonshire Association of Particular Baptist churches. At this point, he was not yet baptised as a believer, which took place in 1783. These men together with others like Robert Hall, Sr. (1728–1791) and John Ryland, Jr. were to become his firm friends. Carey discovered that the Calvinistic theology of the Association echoed his own growing convictions derived from the study of the scriptures.

The Earls Barton congregation asked him to become their pastor but following wise counsel given to him by Sutcliff, Carey declined and became a member of the Baptist church at Olney. Sutcliff's concern was that Carey be sent into the ministry by an orderly church of Christ. The church in Olney tested his gifts but it was not until 1786 that the church was prepared to recognise that he was called to the ministry and send him out to preach the gospel. In August 1787, Fuller, Ryland, and Sutcliff took part in Carey's ordination service.

The church at Moulton was poor and Carey had to work hard as a schoolteacher and as a cobbler to supplement his income and so feed his growing family of three boys. Even then, however, his flair for languages was coming to the fore. With help from Sutcliff, he was acquiring a working knowledge of Latin, Hebrew, and Greek. If that was not enough for this busy man, he was learning in addition Dutch, French, and Italian.

---

[27] While Carey was in Leicester, he was given access to the library of the Philosophical Institute, which was also full of scientific equipment, and the personal libraries of Dr. Thomas Arnold (1742–1816) and Robert Brewin (1741–1821). Carey enjoyed the academic stimulation derived from these contacts. One of his most valuable acquisitions he made was the gift of a book from Arnold on emotional disturbance. At that point he had no idea how valuable that book and that contact would be, given that Dorothy, his first wife, was to suffer severely from a prolonged bout of insanity once in India. See Appleby, *I can plod*, 77, 162–164; Carey, *William Carey*, 63–64; James R. Beck, *Dorothy Carey: The Tragic and Untold Story of Mrs. William Carey* (Grand Rapids, MI: Baker, 1992).

It was Carey's Calvinism which shaped his theology, principles, and priorities during the crucial years prior to 1793 and his departure for Bengal. However, Carey had been brought up as a child of the established Church of England, not as a dissenter and certainly not a Baptist. His father had been the parish clerk and schoolmaster of Paulerspury, where Carey was born in 1761. As one who regularly attended the parish church services, Carey imbibed a general knowledge of the scriptures from an early age. Carey noted that "it is still to me a matter of thankfulness that I had a general knowledge of the bible when I was a child."[28] He read *Pilgrims Progress*, but to no purpose other than the enjoyment of a good story. Much more to his liking were science and travel books, as he read Daniel Defoe's (c.1660–1731) *Robinson Crusoe* (1719) and the *Life of Christopher Columbus*. In fact, he read any books he could find about lands, peoples, languages, and natural history. His uncle, Peter Carey, had returned from military service in Canada with tales which fascinated his young nephew. He also instilled into him a love of gardens and flowers. Carey was to pursue these latter interests in India. His letters home often contained requests not only for books, but for bulbs and seeds together with strict instructions on how they were to be packaged and sent.

Carey reached a turning point in his life when his father apprenticed him to a cobbler in Piddington. There was another apprentice there called John Warr, who was a dissenter. A loyal and proud churchman, Carey had always regarded such people with contempt. Warr engaged Carey in conversation, lent him some books, which are unknown, and left Carey feeling increasingly uneasy, so he decided to leave off sins like lying and swearing. However, he said he had no knowledge of the wickedness of his heart and the necessity of a Saviour. Two further events led to Carey's conversion. First, was his failed attempt to pass off a counterfeit coin to his employer. On being discovered his dishonesty brought over him a sense of shame and disgrace. Secondly, he met with the parish clerk for some six hours discussion on various religious subjects. Carey, reflecting later on this meeting, thought the man possessed divine grace but had strong mystical tendencies. He recorded, "he frequently addressed me with tears in his eyes, in a manner to which I had been unaccustomed, and controverted all my received opinions, which I still think were in the main the doctrines of the gospel, I was affected in a manner which to me was new … I could neither believe his system of doctrines nor defend my own."[29]

The effects of this long conversation, the testimony of Warr, and the exposure of his dishonesty were important steps for Carey. Over the next two years he came "to depend on a crucified Saviour; and to seek a system of doctrines in the word of God."[30] Furthermore having become friends with Warr he began to attend the prayer meetings with the Independent congregation. Not long afterwards he left the Church of England and in 1781 became one of the founding members of the

---

[28] Carey, *Memoir of William Carey*, 18.

[29] Carey, *Memoir of William Carey*, 13–14.

[30] Carey, *Memoir of William Carey*, 14.

Independent church in Hackleton, which eventually became Hackleton Baptist Church.

Following his conversion Carey still struggled but his perplexities drove him back to the Bible. Yet he also found help from a number of different sources. One of them was Thomas Scott (1741–1821), author of *The Force of Truth* (1779), who succeeded John Newton (1725–1807) of Olney in 1781. He met Carey and was very impressed with his conduct and bearing. It was Scott's preaching that was so much help to Carey. Many years later Carey recorded "if there be anything of the work of God in my soul, I owe much of it to Mr Scott's preaching, when I first set out in the ways of the Lord."[31]

A second and very significant source was originally placed in Carey's hands by Thomas Skinner (d. 1795), a Baptist pastor in Towcester. This book was *Help to Zion's Travellers* by Robert Hall, Sr. Peter J. Morden suggests that this book "was probably the most important extra-biblical book that Carey read."[32] Carey's testimony seems to be in agreement:

> I found all that arranged and illustrated which I had been so long picking up as scraps. I do not remember ever to have read any book with such raptures as I did that. If it was poison, as some then said, it was so sweet to me that I drank it greedily to the bottom of the cup; and I rejoice to say, that those doctrines are the choice of my heart to this day.[33]

Hall soon became Carey's spiritual father. He helped him with the composition of his sermons and gave him advice about the pastoral ministry and about his own walk with God. Carey always spoke about his relationship with Hall with deep emotion. After Hall's death in 1791, Carey said of their brief friendship that it was "a jewel I could not too highly prize."[34] Ryland's later comments highlight the significance of Hall's *Help to Zion's Travellers* to Carey:

> here ... [he] first found his own system of divinity. Raised from the greatest obscurity, Mr *Carey* had but little access to books, at his first setting out in religion; and perplexed between the statements of the *Arminians*, and the crudest representations of Calvinism, by persons bordering closely on *Antinomianism*, he searched the Scriptures attentively for himself, endeavouring to find the narrow way, between extremes which seemed irreconcilable to the honour of the divine *government*, and the glory of divine *grace*: and this was the first summary of evangelical truth, which appeared to him fully to accord with the

---

[31] Quoted in Carey, *William Carey*, 33.

[32] Peter J. Morden, *Offering Christ to the World: Andrew Fuller (1754–1815) and the Revival of Eighteenth-Century Particular Baptist Life* (Carlisle: Paternoster, 2003), 181.

[33] Carey, *Memoir of William Carey*, 16–17.

[34] Quoted in Haykin, *One Heart and One Soul*, 93.

sacred standard.[35]

Hall's work dealt with some of the hot issues of the day such as Socinianism, Antinomianism, and the "modern question." Hall came to embrace a warm and systematic evangelical Calvinism, rejecting the high Calvinism that had earlier permeated his own thinking and the thinking of some other Particular Baptists. To read Hall was a defining moment in Carey's life and Hall's *Help to Zion's Travellers* became a lifetime companion. He took it to India, and it was found among his personal possessions after his death. He added his own notes and summaries, and his personal copy is now in possession of the library of Bristol Baptist College.

Hall's book represented the Calvinism of the Northamptonshire Association that sent Carey to India. That same Calvinism was more fully expressed in *The Gospel Worthy of All Acceptation*, the famous book of Andrew Fuller, which was published in 1785. Carey would continue to read Fuller once he had settled in India.

Robert Hall had read carefully the works of Jonathan Edwards (1703–1758) and sermons by John Smalley (1734–1820), one of Edwards' successors. The works of Edwards and his successors had a profound effect on Hall's and Carey's generation of Particular Baptists, and especially on Fuller. There are several indications that Carey also read Edwards extensively and that he continued to do so once he had left England. For example, Carey on reading *The most High a Prayer hearing God* by Edwards exclaimed appreciatively in his journal: "What a spirit of genuine piety flows through all that great Man's Works."[36] Almost ten years before Carey went to India, the association implemented the call to prayer expressed in Edwards' *Humble Attempt*. Churches were meeting for an hour once a month on a Monday evening to pray for the revival of religion and the advancement of God's kingdom on earth. This was closely linked to Edwards' postmillennial eschatology, a view shared by Carey and his friends, and based on a particular interpretation of scriptural promises and prophecies of the last time. Carey in particular was convinced that nothing could ever be accomplished to the glory of God apart from constant dependence on God in prayer. He wrote: "Let us then ever be united in prayer at stated seasons whatever distance may separate us, and let each one of us lay it upon his heart that we will seek to be fervent in spirit, wrestling with God, till he famish these idols and cause the heathen to experience the blessedness that is in Christ."[37]

David Brainerd (1718–1747) was an American missionary to the native Americans who had a particularly fruitful ministry among the Lenape people in New Jersey. During his short life, he was beset by many difficulties. As a result

---

[35] John Ryland, "Recommendatory Preface to the Second London Edition," in Robert Hall, *Help to Zion's Travellers* (Boston: Lincoln, Edmunds and Co., 1833), x.

[36] Carter, ed., *Letters of William Carey*, 22. Other references to Edwards, see Carter, ed., *Letters of William Carey*, 12, 18, 37.

[37] Oussoren, *William Carey*, 283.

of his labours, his biography became a source of inspiration and encouragement to many Christians, including Carey. Edwards was responsible for publishing the account of Brainerd's life. The examples and devotion of Brainerd, the earlier "apostle to the Indians" John Elliot (1604–1690), and the eighteenth-century Moravian missionaries fuelled Carey's passion for taking the gospel to the heathen nations of his day. It was notes from Moravian missionary publications that Carey brought with him to Kettering in 1792 in order to persuade his friends that they too must act in obedience to the command of Christ. Later, Carey adapted and used Moravian practices he had read about. So, for example, in agreement with Marshman and Ward, they lived with their families together as a community, sharing everything together as one family. All these features found their way into Carey's *Enquiry* and into the "Serampore Form of Agreement." S. Pearce Carey recorded the significance of Elliot and Brainerd to Carey, "he learned how the one had toiled with a scholar's patience and an apostle's grace for nearly sixty years amongst America's Indians, and had been the first to translate the whole Bible into a pagan tongue; and how the other, in three seraphic years had burned himself out for these Indians and God. Thence-forward these, with Paul, were his canonized heroes."[38] Carey continued to read and re-read Brainerd once he had arrived in India. Above all, he admired and desired to imitate Brainerd's self-sacrifice in his service of Christ. He later urged his missionary colleagues, "Let us often look at Brainerd, in the woods of America, pouring out his very soul before God for the perishing heathen, without whose salvation nothing could make him happy. Prayer secret, fervent, believing prayer, lies at the root of all godliness."[39]

One other name that appears in Carey's *Enquiry* was Captain James Cook (1728–1779), an explorer and navigator. Given Carey's great interest in travel books it was not surprising that he borrowed and read of Cook's voyages especially to the Pacific Ocean. Cook's description of different places stirred Carey to pray for the heathen. God used these volumes to touch Carey's heart. He looked beyond the adventures. When he read these accounts in 1783, they turned Carey's mind to think of missions. Mary, Carey's sister, testified,

> He was always, from his first being thoughtful, remarkably impressed about heathen lands and the slave trade. I never remember him engaging in prayer, in his family or in public, without praying for those poor creatures. The first time I ever recollect my feeling for the heathen world, was from a discourse I heard my brother preach at Moulton ... it was a day to be remembered by me.[40]

These then were some of the books which moulded Carey's theology, missionary practices, and his translation priorities. The picture of Carey and his books would

---

[38] Carey, *William Carey*, 51.

[39] Oussoren, *William Carey*, 283.

[40] Quoted in Appleby, *I can plod*, 50.

be incomplete if we did not consider a pamphlet bearing Carey's name which first appeared in the spring of 1792. Ernest Payne says of Carey's *Enquiry into the Obligations of Christians to use means for the Conversion of the Heathen*, that it "may rightly be regarded as a landmark in Christian history."[41] Michael A.G. Haykin stated that it "would prove to be as seminal a work as Fuller's *The Gospel Worthy of All Acceptation*."[42] Therefore we turn to briefly consider this landmark publication.

Carey's Enquiry

Carey's slim volume, as it was less than ninety pages, was eight or nine years in the making. He was very reluctant to put anything into print and urged Fuller and Sutcliff to publish something. They refused and instead encouraged Carey. He was only twenty-seven when he finally decided to publish it. Anyone reading the *Enquiry* and who is acquainted with the subsequent life of this man will not be surprised at what they find. Much of what he was as a man and the secret of what he achieved under God in India is found in its pages. Carey was above all else driven by a desire for the glory of God.

Sections II and III of Carey's *Enquiry* had perhaps been longest in the making. Section II traced the history of missions down to the late eighteenth century and was the fruit of Carey's own reading. Reading was also the source for Section III. It was a statistical survey of all the countries of the then-known world, information he had gathered by ransacking travel books, geographical handbooks and the local paper, the *Northampton Mercury*. He had begun to collate this data on maps and his leather globe in his cobbler's workshop. In his summary comments Carey records,

> It must undoubtedly strike every considerate mind, what a vast proportion of the sons of Adam there are, who yet remain in the most deplorable state of heathen darkness, without any means of knowing the true God, except what are afforded them by the works of nature; and utterly destitute of the knowledge of the gospel of Christ, or of any means of obtaining it. In many of these countries they have no written language, consequently no Bible, and are only led by the most childish customs and traditions.[43]

In Section I Carey set out to demolish the objections raised by high Calvinism to bringing the gospel to the nations. It was often suggested by them that the mandate to evangelise the world was limited to the apostles and that it had been fulfilled in their lifetime. Carey's answer was simple. He turned directly to Matt 28:18–20 and argued that if the command to evangelise the world applied only to the apostles, then so did the command to baptise, which was a strong argument to use among

---

[41] Ernest A. Payne, "Introduction" in William Carey, *An Enquiry into the Obligations of Christians to Use Means for the Conversion of the Heathen* (London: Carey Kingsgate, 1961), i.

[42] Haykin, *One Heart and One Soul*, 189.

[43] Carey, *Enquiry*, 62–63.

his fellow Baptists. That being the case, anyone who had gone to other nations and preached and planted other churches had no authorization from Christ to do so. Finally, he pointed out that the promised continual presence of Christ made little sense if the task had actually been completed by the apostles. Here was Carey demonstrating from scripture that missionary work was the present duty of the church. In the title, he used the word "obligation," meaning missionary work was a bounden duty, a matter of obedience to the mandate of Jesus Christ.

In Section IV he tackled the practical objections that had been raised by his proposals and showed effectively that they really were nothing more than excuses. Finally in Section V he considered the duty and the means that were to be used to promote this great undertaking. He placed "fervent and united prayer" for the working of the Holy Spirit as being of first priority. Carey's own stress on the importance of prayer and the monthly prayer meetings among the churches of the association explain why this was a priority for Carey.

But Carey knew something had to be done in order to "the obtaining of those things we pray for."[44] Drawing on the analogy of trading companies who organised themselves to go to the utmost limits to secure material wealth, he asked why could not a company of serious Christians form a society with a committee to oversee the gathering of information, the collection of funds, and the selecting and training of other missionaries. He concluded by referring to Gal 6:7--whatever a man sows, that he will also reap. What a harvest he said,

> await such characters as *Paul*, and *Elliot*, and *Brainerd*, and others, who have given themselves wholly to the work of the Lord. What a heaven will it be to see the many myriads of poor heathens, of Britons amongst the rest, who by their labours have been brought to the knowledge of God. Surely a *crown of rejoicing* like this is worth aspiring to. Surely it is worth while to lay ourselves out with all our might, in promoting the cause, and the kingdom of Christ.[45]

Within a year of the publication of the pamphlet, William Carey was making arrangements to sail to India. In June 1793 he finally set sail with his family and John Thomas. Andrew Fuller rejoiced in the way God had brought about this event. Writing to another supporter of the mission he said of Carey now, "he will live and die in the midst of hundreds of millions of heathens, for whose salvation I am sure he is ready to sacrifice his life, and a thousand lives if he had them."[46]

One lesson from Carey
Ezra was "a skilled scribe" (Ezra 7:6). The imprisoned apostle urged Timothy to bring "the books and especially the parchments" (2 Tim 4:13) when he

---

[44] Carey, *Enquiry*, 81.

[45] Carey, *Enquiry*, 87.

[46] Quoted in Haykin, *One Heart and One Soul*, 235.

came. In such men as these Carey would have found kindred spirits. Jesus Christ affirmed that "every scribe instructed concerning the kingdom of heaven is like a householder who brings out of his treasure things new and old" (Matt 13:52). Carey loved the scriptures and the doctrines of grace, and so was well-instructed concerning the kingdom of heaven. He was a life-long student. Books were always on his desk. He became an avid and disciplined reader and re-read key books. It is not therefore surprising that on leaving England for India he proved to be a faithful "householder," reading, translating, writing, preaching, and applying the Scriptures in a very different and demanding environment. His life displayed a consistent, persevering, earnest, and single-minded determination to serve Christ with cheerful obedience. For over forty years in India, he maintained a disciplined daily and weekly routine of reading, study, and writing. By so doing William Carey eventually gave the Indian sub-continent the Scriptures in many different languages.

He was first and foremost a man of the Bible. As an ardent student of the Scriptures, he also became a student of many other books, a multi-disciplinary scholar of note. By using such means the truth of God's gospel was clarified in Carey's thinking: he was instructed; he was humbled; yet, he was also stimulated and fired up to serve Christ and the cause of truth. The importance of Christians continuing to read, study, and, if possible, to write good books should be shouted from the rooftops. By his own admission, Carey was a plodder. "I can plod," he told Eustace Carey, "I can persevere in any definite pursuit. To this I owe everything."[47] Carey did persevere, using the means at his disposal to be instructed, humbled, stimulated, and fired up to follow Christ. Can we do less, whatever the measure of our gifts?

---

[47] Carey, *Memoir of William Carey*, 623.

Texts and documents

Thomas Williams' letter

Initial edit by Ron Downing; revised ed. & intro. Michael A.G. Haykin

Michael A.G. Haykin is Professor of Church History and Director, The Andrew Fuller Center for Baptist Studies at The Southern Baptist Theological Seminary, Louisville, KY.

Introduction

Thomas Williams (1757–1805) was the founding pastor of Eastcombe Baptist Church, Gloucestershire. He began preaching in the village of Eastcombe in the summer of 1799. Within two years, a small congregation had been formed and grew to be over 40 members by 1805 with some 500 regularly coming to hear Williams preach in a chapel that was erected in 1800–1801. He wrote the following letter to the church and congregation on March 16, 1805, during his final illness. I have added the paragraph divisions in the letter.[1]

Text

Brethren, Friends and Neighbours,

These last three Lord's days I have been laid aside from my public work among you, through the afflicting hand of God on my tottering unworthy tabernacle; but I can assure you it has been, and is now, the sweetest affliction I ever knew in the whole of my life. Christ was never so precious, so valuable, so lovely, so glorious, so amiable as now. I hope never to my last moment never to lose the savour of that

---

[1] This letter is adopted from Ron Downing, ed., "Eastcombe Baptist Church," accessed July 16, 2023, https://www.genuki.org.uk/big/eng/GLS/Eastcombe/ebc-notes.

communion I had with Him the greater part of last Tuesday week, and which lasted until midnight. The pleasure was so great I have not words to convey my feelings. In fact, I found so much of heaven in my soul, that it appeared to me I was nearly wafted to the skies, and had it not been for my dear afflicted wife and family, and my dear mournful flock, I should much more than preferred leaving this world of misery and sin, and to be for ever with my dear Lord and Saviour. But it seems as if the Master intended to continue me longer with you, how long no one can tell, but when I consider that my constitution is so much broken (and blessed be God, broken in His service and work, and not in the service of Satan) my time in this world must be short. May I and each of you improve every moment to His honour and glory.

Whenever I reflect upon that providence, which brought, and has kept me amongst you for nearly six years, in which time a spacious building has been erected for the public worship of God, for you, and your children for ever, who can help exclaiming, 'What Hath God wrought,' and especially when I consider the number of Church Members, which is now 46, with the agreeable prospect of several others to join that number as soon as it shall please God to establish my health. Next to going to heaven I long for the day. May the Holy Spirit be with the Candidates, as with the Master when He came up out of Jordan's flood. You know my friends, that we have, enjoyed His favour on these occasions, and I think we shall again. This will cause another shout amongst the angels in heaven, and we will join the triumph with them, though we are still on earth.

Oh, what a friend is Christ How good His work, how sweet His employ, how glorious His wages! May Christ ever enable you to adorn your profession. It has afforded me abundance of pleasure to see this house so well attended, and especially so many young persons hearing the word of life with so much seriousness. But what joy it would give me if all were willing to follow the Lamb, for that would at once cure all of the love of sin. I have thought lately if it were possible to mourn in heaven, I should weep exceedingly if ever the cause of Christ were to decline at Eastcombe. I pray God there may be a large number of godly, pious, faithful souls here as long as the sun and moon endure.

I conclude, wishing that the heavens may be opened, and pour blessings upon you and your children.

From your affectionate Minister, Thomas Williams.

"We Want Love": College Lane Church's letter to the Northamptonshire Association

ed. Garrett M. Walden

Garrett Walden is a pastor at Grace Heritage Church in Auburn, Alabama. He's married to Kat, and they have four children. In addition to his regular preaching ministry at his church, he's an editor for The London Lyceum. He has a ThM from The Southern Baptist Theological Seminary.

Introduction

The Northamptonshire Baptist Association, perhaps most famous for birthing the Baptist Missionary Society in 1792, has much to teach contemporary Baptists as they consider their bases of partnership. What should be the doctrinal foundations upon which their cooperative efforts stand? What duties do the churches have toward one another? Answers to such questions have evolved over time, but there is wisdom in looking to the past.

What follows is the letter from College Lane Church to the Northamptonshire Association, which met in Olney in 1768.[1] It is well known that the annual association meetings resulted in a circular letter to be published and distributed among the churches. However, it is also the case that each of the member churches sent a letter with their messengers to be read and discussed at the annual meeting—something like a brief "state of the church" address. Such letters are not as readily accessible, but below is the letter to the association from the pen of John Collett Ryland (1723–1792), pastor of the College Lane Church in Northampton. My transcription retains the spellings, punctuation, and capitalization as it appears in the church book.

---

[1] This letter is found on pages 71–83 in the College Lane Church, Northampton church book. I am indebted to Rev. Tim Stanyon for assisting me in archival research. See "Church book," B/CSBC/047, Northamptonshire Archives and Heritage, Northampton. Spelling, punctuation, and capitalization have been left as in the original.

Text
The first Letter to the Association at Olney meeting June 15. 1768
To the Elders and Brethren of the several Gospel Churches, professing the rich and glorious and comfortable Doctrines of eternal, absolute and personal Election to Holiness and Happiness Original Guilt and universal Depravation of the Soul—particular and unconditional Redemption by the Death of Christ—free Justification by the imputed Righteousness of Christ alone—Efficacious Grace in the Regeneration of the Soul, and undoubted invincible Preservation in Grace to the final Salvation of the Soul, met in an Association at Olney in Buckinghamshire On Wednesday June 15. 1768

The Church of Christ meeting in College Lane Northampton, of the same Faith, Worship and discipline sendeth cordial and respectful salutation

Beloved Brethren in our glorious Lord and Head Jesus Christ.

We are drawn by the Force of true Brotherly Love, and excited by a Zeal against the Principles and Actions of the Enemies of the Gospel to meet you in this your annual Association. We believe you will not assemble together to exercise any Dominion over our Consciences and our Faith but merely to consult our best Interests and promote our highest Happiness and upon these Principles and Views we esteem and honour you, and desire your most fervent and united Prayers for our Comfort and Joy in the Lord.

In the present Day we have all the Reason in the World to cleave to the People of GOD, that spiritual and blessed Body who are beloved by GOD the Father, redeemed by GOD the Son, and sanctified by GOD the Holy Ghost, and who are infallibly to make a Part of God's blessed and triumphant Empire for evermore.

Thanks be to our GOD in Covenant notwithstanding the Socinians of the present Day are using all the Craft and Malice they are possessed of to darken the Glory of the Gospel, to rob the Lord Jesus of his true and proper Divinity—banish the blessed Spirit from the Churches, and destroy the Salvation of every Man in the World.—We say this to the Honour of sovereign and absolute Grace, we have been preserved from the dreadful and growing Apostasy and are in the full Possession of the Doctrines, Ordinances, & Privileges of the Gospel and to our Joy we see the Pleasure that God takes in the Salvation of Sinners, and the Work of Conversion going forward amongst us.

We have had thirteen added to us since the last association and through Grace a prospect of several more—We are in peace amongst Ourselves—and but a very few there be who walk disorderly—We have lost Two Men by Death, but blessed be GOD we have good Hope that they are both gone to Heaven.[2]

We may reasonably expect from Persons of your sublime Principles and endowed with such rich and eternal Privileges many things to be done for the Interest and Good of the Churches you represent.

---

[2] A marginal note reads: "Two Dead in this year [/] William Brooks March 1768 [/] Richard Beck April 1768"

We expect from you the fundamental Duty of Love, fervent Love, deep Love not superficial, hearty Love, not in pretence,—active Love, not a meer saying be ye spiritually warmed, be ye filled with the Fullness of God—No Dear sirs we want Love that appears in substantial and generous Actions and Prayers. We want you to wrestle with GOD for us, and to give him no Rest till he has established Jerusalem and made his Church the Praise of the whole Earth.—We want your Sympathy with Us in all our Afflictions—your Pity in all our Troubles—your Compassion in all our Crosses and Tryals of Life.

Dear Brethren do not disappoint our hopes, do not be like a Summer Brook to fail us in our greatest Times of Need. Don't give us Occasion to reproach you with loving us only in Word and flattering Pretences but not in Deed and in Truth.

We all join in requesting that the Association may be at Northampton next year, and we hope you will appoint your Time to be either some Day in May or in July because our Minister being obliged to be absent always in the Month of June he could not have the Profit and Pleasure of enjoying your Company.

We likewise desire another Favour and which is of great Consequence to us and to the other Brethren who may attend upon the services of that Day—It is that our Preachers would particularly state and defend the great Doctrines of the GODHEAD and Satisfaction of Christ, with the Work of the Holy Ghost in Regeneration and the Sanctification of the Souls of Men in order to their eternal Happiness[3]

As the Ministers and People in the Socinian Scheme, are active and unwearied in their Endeavours to propagate and spread their destructive Notions thro' all parts of this Kingdom, and even amongst the People in North America,—We would earnestly desire that you would join with us in imitating Socinian Diligence but apply that Diligence to the glorious Purposes of defending and spreading the Glorious Gospel of the blessed GOD,—shall Men who take a vast deal of Pains to damn their own Souls, outdo us in Activity? Heaven forbid!—And we can just now congratulate you and Ourselves, on a fresh prospect of the Divine Wisdom and Faithfulness at this critical Time of daring Error and Blasphemy, when the Enemies of Christ have exceeded all former Ages in Rudeness and unblushing Impudence—We rejoice with you O! ye honoured Servants of the Lord Jesus, to see that he is now by his Providence, giving to his Churches a Work which is the Result of Fifty Years close Study of the Sacred Scriptures, and which we hope you will expressly recommend as well in your Pulpits, as in your printed Circular Letter of the present year.[4]

---

[3] The association accommodated Ryland's two requests, and they met at the end of May 1769 in Northampton. Ryland was asked to author the association's annual circular letter on the theme of the Holy Spirit's work in sanctification, which he entitled, *The Assistance of God to True Christians*.

[4] This forthcoming work is likely a reference to Ryland's own supplement to the Presbyterian minister, John Leland's (1691–1766) work against the Deists, which first appeared in two volumes in 1754–1755 entitled, *A View of the Principal Deistical Writers that Have Appeared in England in the Last and Present Century*. It was Leland's work that was fifty years in the making, according to Ryland. Ryland's work was not

And now Dear Brethren, May Grace Mercy and Peace from GOD our Father and the LORD Jesus Christ be with you whilst assembled, and when you shall be returned to your respective Congregations,—We remain

Your affectionate Brethren and servant in the LORD

John Ryland

Signed by Us at our Church Meeting June 12. 1768 in Behalf of the Whole.

---

ready for advertisement in the 1768 circular letter as he requested, but it was advertised at the end of the 1769 associational circular letter (which Ryland wrote). See John Ryland, *The Scheme of Infidelity Ruined For Ever: or, The Deistical and Socinian Schemes Demonstrated to be Insufficient for the Happiness of Mankind; and the Necessity of the Glorious Gospel to Discover Pardon, Sanctification, and Support in Death* (London: E. and C. Dilly, 1770).

"I had far rather take one convert from Satan, than a thousand from a brother": James Hinton on Protestant catholicity[1]

ed. Chance Faulkner

Chance Faulkner serves as a Junior Fellow of the Andrew Fuller Center for Baptist Studies and is a MTh candidate at Union School of Theology in Wales.

Introduction

The city of Oxford in the eighteenth century was a breeding ground of suspicion and disdain towards dissenters by the "university-bred Anglicans," as one of the two training centres for the Establishment.[2] William Pitt (1759–1806) described the established church as "so essential part of the constitution that whatever endangered it would necessarily affect the security of the whole."[3] Dissenters were looked upon as "schismatical" and "tainted with militarism," accused of holding the same views that led to the French Revolution, and therefore seen and treated as a threat to its security.[4] Therefore, as Walters Stevens rightly notes, "Only the stouthearted with firmly-grounded convictions could survive in this atmosphere."[5]

Not long after James Hinton (1761–1823) arrived in Oxford, for example, Edward Tatham (1749–1834), the rector of Lincoln College, went on a preaching

---

[1] This letter is extracted from John Howard Hinton, *A Biographical Portraiture of the late Rev. James Hinton, M.A.* (Oxford: Bartlett and Hinton; London: B.J. Holdsworth, 1824), 323–325. Capitalization and spelling have been modernized.

[2] Walter Stevens, "Oxford's Attitude to Dissenters, 1646–1946," *Baptist Quarterly* 13.1 (1949): 4.

[3] J. Rule, *Albion's People: English Society 1714–1815* (London: 1992), 93. Cited in Nigel Yates, "The Threat of Revolution," in *Eighteenth-Century Britain, 1714–1815* (Edinburgh: Pearson, 2008), 177.

[4] Stevens, "Oxford's Attitude to Dissenters," 8, 5; Hinton, *Biographical Portraiture*, 259, 349.

[5] Stevens, "Oxford's Attitude to Dissenters," 6.

tour in Oxford attacking dissenters—particularly Hinton and his congregation. These sermons were published and went through eight printings in the first year.[6] A few years later, in 1794, Hinton was mobbed at the riot at Woodstock and barely escaped with his life.[7] It is no wonder that Joseph Ivimey (1773–1834) said that Hinton "was called to fill perhaps one of the most difficult stations in which a nonconformist minister, in England, could have been placed."[8]

It is in light of this context that makes the following letter, written to a minister in the Church of England, so remarkable. Hearing there is an evangelical church in the city of Oxford, Hinton desires to support, encourage, and fellowship with them. It was his desire that the evangelical churches had harmony and peace together. Hinton had no wish to make his chief aim a Baptist (or even dissenting) cause, but that men and women would find a place where the gospel was preached. He had no intention of winning other believers over to his own second or tertiary sentiments (e.g. baptism or church government), but to see men and women brought to and flourish in Christ—whether Baptist, Presbyterian, Methodists, or even the Church of England.

For Hinton, it was better to worship and fellowship with believers who differ in form but who are people of the gospel, than to worship with a church who has forsaken its truth and power. He aims to love all who love the Lord Jesus Christ and support them in any way, even if it means discretely from afar—as a connection to dissenters could stain the reputation of the minister's church and ministry. "Gospel ministers, of every name, are but few," says Hinton "and I most heartily wish them all good speed in the name of the Lord. I wish to allure to every net, and to see the partners 'fill both the ships,' knowing well that at last thousands will elude all their skill." Gospel integrity, for Hinton, is not just a matter of believing the right things, but living in light of their reality—including living in harmony with all those who love the Lord Jesus Christ. In this letter, we see Protestant catholicity at its best.

Text

So much do we value the substance above the form, that, whenever it appears that gospel truth is forsaken in any of our pulpits, the hearers uniformly seek it wherever it may be found. I could just as soon advise my people to leave off prayer, or any other duty of the Christian life, as to refrain from hearing the gospel at

---

[6] Edward Tatham, *A Sermon Suitable to the Times, Preached at St. Mary's, Oxford, on Sunday the 18th at St. Martins's, on Sunday the 25th of November at St. Peters in the East, on Sunday the 2s; at All Saints, on Sunday the 9th; a d at St. Mary Magdalen' on Sunday the 16th of December* (London: J.F. and C. Rivington; Oxford: J.F. Fletcher, J. Cooke, and R. Bliss, 1792).

[7] For more on the Woodstock Riot, see Michael A.G. Haykin, *"Accounted worthy to bear in my body the marks of the Lord Jesus": James Hinton, the persecution of English Dissent, & the Woodstock Riot*, Occasional Publication No. 8 (Louisville, KY: Andrew Fuller Center for Baptist Studies, 2018). This is also reprinted and slightly edited as "James Hinton (1761–1823)," in *The British Particular Baptists*, ed. Michael A.G. Haykin and Terry Wolever (Springfield, MO: Particular Baptist Press, 2020), 5:374–399.

[8] Joseph Ivimey, *The Excellence and Utility of an Evangelical Ministry, as Exercised by Protestant Dissenters* (London: John Offor, 1823), A2.

church, when they cannot hear it in their own place of worship. As much as the wheat is preferable to the husk that contains it, or a jewel to the casket in which it is held, is the gospel itself preferable to all the forms in which it is displayed. With the gospel, Christ will save souls; without it, they are forever lost. Forms are all temporal; truth is eternal. Gospel ministers, of every name, are but few, and I most heartily wish them all good speed in the name of the Lord. I wish to allure to every net, and to see the partners "fill both the ships," knowing well that at last thousands will elude all their skill.

I have heard a pious clergyman say publicly, "If the gospel were faithfully preached in our churches, the meeting-houses would be empty." Alas, my dear sir, why should he be so eager to empty meeting-houses? Why not first empty public-houses, gaming-houses, and play-houses? Why not invade Satan's kingdom? I have tried if I could possibly wish to empty a church where a Cadogan or a Robinson preached?[9] No: from my heart I believe God would be offended dreadfully with the wish. I had far rather take one convert from Satan, than a thousand from a brother. I have no wish to make proselytes of true Christians. I wish their love, but I wish them also to continue their support to their own pastors. The world is wide enough for us all. "If thou take to the right, then I will take to the left; but let there be no strife, I pray thee, between me and thee" [Gen 13:8]. Such has been the tendency of all my conduct. In Oxford prudence is especially necessary; and if it appears to you that a cordial understanding between us, would promote the great objects, the peace and prosperity of the gospel, you may lay our intercourse under whatever restrictions you think proper. I know my situation and yours. Had I opportunity for free conversation, I should propose some method to prevent the misrepresentations to which we are liable, from mutual hearers or acquaintances. I know my people think as I do, and study peace: throw your influence into the same scale, and the work is done. In a word, whatever, consistently with the duty I owe to the sacredness of truth, and to that of my ministerial office (which neither of us must for a moment degrade) can be suggested to render our congregations harmonious, our labours more useful, and the prospect of our interview with our flocks at the day of God more delightful, will suit the wishes of, Rev. sir,

Yours most sincerely to serve in Christ.
[James Hinton]

---

[9] William Bromley Cadogan (1751–1797) was an Anglican Minister and successor of William Talbot at St. Giles, Reading and also St. Lukes, Chelsea. He came to evangelical views after an illness in 1782. See Arthur Pollard, "Cadogan, Hon. William Bromley," in *Dictionary of Evangelical Biography, 1730–1860*, ed. Donald M. Lewis (Peabody, MA: Hendrickson, 2004), 1:182. Thomas Robinson (1749–1813) was an evangelical vicar of St Mary's, Leicester. For more on Robinson, see Edward Thomas Vaughan, *Some Account of the Reverend Thomas Robinson, M.A. Late Vicar of St. Mary's, Leicester, and Sometime Fellow of Trinity College, Cambridge: with a Selection of Original Letters* (London: Sherwood, Neely, and Jones, 1816); J.H. Lupton, "Robinson, Thomas (1749–1813)" in *Dictionary of National Biography*, ed. Leslie Stephen (London, 1897), 49:52–53.

Book Reviews

Charles H. Parker, *Global Calvinism: Conversion and Commerce in the Dutch Empire, 1600–1800* (New Haven: Yale University Press, 2022), 408 pages.

In his new book *Global Calvinism*, professor of history at Saint Louis University, Charles H. Parker, offers a significant contribution to the field of global history. Parker explores a wide breadth of archival sources alongside published primary and secondary sources as he engages with a variety of fields such as history, theology, linguistics, and ethnography. This work sheds light onto influence of Dutch Calvinism on global discussions through their engagement with commerce from the 1600–1800. It was thus not a monolithic European ideology, but one that was shaped through dialogue with different religions, cultures, and languages.

The book is organized into six main chapters. The first chapter charts the expansion of the Dutch empire throughout the world and includes maps which detail the trade routes they established in different areas. These show how their trading outposts became places where the Dutch would look to establish Calvinistic influences, and by extension the realities faced by the missions engaged at these locations.

Chapter two displays how the Calvinist ministers would serve "colonial needs in creating an educated local population and reducing crime, disorder, and unrest" (p.69). Parker surveys the ideology of Hugo Grotius before looking at some of the conflicts that existed between the local colonial trading posts and the Calvinist ministers serving there. He also looks at three specific areas in which Calvinists ministers focused their effort on colonial territories: by promoting their view of marriage and sexuality, by setting up diaconates to help the poor, and in their support of slavery. As Parker points out, "The rationale of Christianizing slaves in a benevolent regime of servitude became the standard language of explanation in justifying the use of slave labor in the colonies" (p.107).

Chapter three considers the Dutch Calvinists' desire and difficulties in converting others to Calvinistic Christianity, noting their efforts to educate others in the reformed tradition via the translation of texts into the native tongue of those to whom they ministered. As many native people would affirm Calvinism to a degree, however, but still hold to their other traditions—some Calvinist clergy created a tier system in the church. While people could be baptized into the church, they could not receive the eucharist until they showed adequate Christian understanding and maturity: "Under this policy, large numbers of Asian converts, almost entire congregations, could claim a Reformed Protestant identity but never took communion" (p.155). This model of ministry caused problems and some criticized this approach as "dividing the sacraments" (p.156).

Chapter four looks at the linguistic considerations of the Calvinists engaging with those of other languages, as well as the controversies that arose around different methods of translation. Although some leaders desired to teach Dutch to those they were ministering to, the majority practice became that ministers would seek to learn the dominant language and minister to the people through that medium. Chapter five analyzes different writings to discern how Reformed Protestants were shaped by their engagement with other religions. It also engages closely with different primary sources and focuses on the thought of Grotius, Uldemans, and Vossius in particular. The analysis provided by Parker shows how interest with world religions was based out of Christian engagement with non-Christians and a subsequent desire to see people convert to Christianity.

Finally, chapter six continues a similar theme, showing the engagement Dutch Calvinists had with other religions. In this chapter Parker focuses more on how other ideologies engaged the perception of Calvinists, placing an emphasis on Cartesianism and rationalism. Parker shows how the Dutch Calvinists thinking was influenced by their global interactions, and therefore their debates at home were understood within these larger global engagements. As Parker states, "Global comparisons gave orthodox Calvinists a new way of seeing their enemies and their intellectual threats" (p.254).

One area of critique is that Parker does at times show a lack of precision regarding theological debates that provide the historical foundations to Reformed thought in the 1600–1800s. Of course, the question of the terminology "Calvinist" and "Reformed" are themselves debated, but Parker here seems to use "Reformed" as a label for the larger movement involving both the counter-Remonstrance and the Remonstrance, and uses the term "Calvinist" specifically as the counter-Remonstrance view. However, Parker's delineation between the two camps requires more nuance. He mentions that Arminius took issue with Gomarius' doctrine that "God had predestined the saved to eternity in heaven and the damned to eternity in hell before he created the world." Following this debate, Parker says the Gomarius' view is the one that would become the orthodox Calvinist position, which argues that "God conferred salvation or damnation on individuals according to his own counsel before creation" (p.31). The presentation here is imprecise. Arminius himself believed that God predestined people "before he created the world," speaking in a chronological sense. However, it may be that Parker has in mind here the order of decrees, that in logical order God decreed predestination first prior to the decree to create the world, thus presenting a supralapsarian position. To be sure, Arminius took issue with supralapsarianism, but to say that supralapsarianism was the view that became the standard of orthodox Calvinism is not accurate. Rather, the Canons of Dordt allowed for both an Infralapsarian and Supralapsarian position.

Thus, a more careful discussion of the soteriological issues at play that led to Dordt and that were agreed upon at Dort would have aided the volume, especially in setting up the difference between the Remonstrance and Counter-Remonstrance (or for Parker, "Calvinist") position.

Overall, however, this is a must-read study for those of varying degrees of familiarity. It will be of particular interest to any scholar engaged in Reformation studies, reformed orthodoxy, or global history of the Christian church. However, it would also be of use to those wanting to learn more about the history of missions and the tensions that existed between colonial expansion and the ministry of the Church outside of the specialization as well.

Jonathan N. Cleland
Knox College
Toronto, ON

Rob Boss, *Thunder God, Wonder God: Exploring the Emblematic Vision of Jonathan Edwards* (LaVergne, TN: Jonathan Edwards Society Press, 2023), 798 pages.

Thunder God, Wonder God by Rob Boss is an expanded version of his *God-Haunted World* (2015). This edition, under new title, features an emblematic anthology integrating other emblematic literature from the early modern era. With a provocative introduction, Boss seeks to help twenty-first century minds to understand Edwards' desire to "re-inscripturate" the world. As the Enlightenment threatened to detach the supernatural from the natural—what Avihu Zakai has called disenchantment—Edwards had sought to reverse course. Gerald McDermott provides a strong foreword for Boss' volume highlighting Edwards' firm belief in a harmony of existence that values the universal, but not at the expense of the particular. This belief led Edwards to think about the similarities of creation as a means of knowing the Creator affectionately. "Re-inscripturating" the world, according to Boss, is Edwards' unique approach to interpreting the natural world through scripture. While this volume may not have a direct correlation to Andrew Fuller, the approach described herein, however, was part of the colorful makeup of Fuller's esteemed theological mentor.

The introduction is a creative adaptation of the Inklings who met at the Eagle and Child pub in Oxford. His cadre of characters include E.O. Wilson, Iain McGilchrist, and Jonathan Edwards. Their discussion serves to illustrate how the human brain has been gifted with the ability to make creative inference between similar or dissimilar structures, patterns, and ideas. A botanist might present factual elements about a rose from a "left brain" perspective and yet a "right brain" person might make associations that transcend the physical. This creative dialogue exposes how emblematic literature seeks to harness the words of God in nature.

The second chapter provides a short history of emblematic literature from the

Renaissance to the early modern era as a worldview. Several persons are highlighted during this period that provide a context for Edwards. These include Andrea Alciati (author of *Emblematum liber*, or Book of Emblems), Martin Luther, John Calvin, Wolfgang Franzius (author of *Historiae animalium sacra*), Conrad Gesner (author of *Historiae animalium*), Edwards Topsell (author of *Historie of Four-Footed Beasts*), and Ulisse Aldrovandi. According to Robert Boss, "de-inscripturation" of the natural world occurred as Galileo emphasized how a mathematical language was necessary to learn what God was saying in creation. In this respect Galileo believed that nature's message was opaque. Any definite message from God ought to be derived from the scriptures.

The third chapter examines the influence of an emblematic worldview upon theology. Here Bishop Joseph Hall, Baptists such as Ralph Austen, John Bunyan, Benjamin Keach, and Congregationalist Cotton Mather are resurrected to demonstrate the meditative tradition which sought to "harness sensuous imagery for spiritual ends" (p.65). The fourth chapter takes the final step to Edwards in which Edwards addresses the Enlightenment project to make the universe a purposeless mechanism. Pushing back against this Deist worldview Edwards' observations about nature are brought to the foreground. Edwards is described as a conservative emblematic writer because he sought to only highlight that which Scripture would support. Boss, then, categorizes these observations by biblical theme in chapter five. Helpful exegetical notes are provided on these themes. After a brief concluding chapter Boss provides Edwards' "Images of Divine Things" alphabetically interposing other emblematic sources for comparison. These include Bunyan, Hall, Alciati, George Wither, Francis Quarles, and Christopher Harvey. In this reviewer's opinion a short "contributing author biography" would be beneficial to contextualize the more obscure authors included.

All things considered this volume has several benefits. First, it not only places modern thinkers into Edwards' *Typological Writings*, but also places Edwards' 212 "Images of Divine Things" into typological thinkers of the Renaissance and early modern period. It seems apparent that the change in interpretive methodology after Galileo, not only affected how people looked at nature, but also how types, symbols, and apocalyptic aspects of scripture were understood more "literally" in the nineteenth century. Second, this volume helps readers understand how *Sinners in the Hands of an Angry God* was notably dynamic. Edwards believed that the famous images from this sermon were imbued with scriptural truth. The images of lions, worms, spiders, bows and arrows, pits and slippery places, and dreadful storms with big thunder were effective because, according to Edwards, they had the voice of God in them. Third, this book will serve scholars who desire to anticipate what *A History of the Work of Redemption* might have looked like if he had been given the chance to compose it. For example, Boss points out that Edwards' tendency to view reality as a "three-story universe that perfectly corresponds to the spiritual world" (p.135) led him to look for the particular in the universal (p.19). This "three-story universe" would likely have served as the structure for his projected *History*. In his letter to the trustees of the College of New Jersey (1757) he referred to this general structure of heaven, earth, and hell in his proposed new method of theological exposition. The emblems found in nature and scripture would have helped color in this three-story presentation. Fourth, the anthology may provide pastors with a vibrant way to engage congregations by using the images in the world to illustrate spiritual truth. There is, according to Edwards, a profundity in the natural world that inherently corresponds to the book of scripture (p.142).

John S. Banks
Vrije Universiteit Amsterdam
The Netherlands

D. Bruce Hindmarsh, *The Spirit of Early Evangelicalism: True Religion in a Modern World* (New York: Oxford University Press, 2018), 354 pages.

For someone who has already enriched the study of evangelicalism, notably regarding John Newton (1725–1807), D. Bruce Hindmarsh has made yet another significant contribution to this vital era of church history with *The Spirit of Early Evangelicalism*. The title is reminiscent of the seminal patristic-era work, *The Spirit of Early Christian Thought* (2003), by Robert Louis Wilken, though Hindmarsh's focus takes on a slightly different form than Wilken's. While Wilken organized his study in theological categories, Hindmarsh has done so according to *cultural* categories. Thus, through the lens of science, art, and law, Hindmarsh not only provides a review of the usual suspects of early evangelicalism like George Whitefield (1714–1770), John Wesley (1703–1791), and Jonathan Edwards (1703–1758), but he also showed how this movement impacted the culture and vice versa. Through this, Hindmarsh seeks to demonstrate how early evangelical spirituality and eighteenth-century culture overlapped with one another, particularly with how evangelical spirituality related to the societal developments of the age in thinking, knowledge, and perspectives on the natural world.

Hindmarsh begins with Whitefield, whom he set forth as an early exemplar of the kind of zealous devotion that would come to characterize evangelicalism. In this first chapter, Whitefield's diary was in focus as it depicted the variety of influences in the young, aspiring preacher's spiritual life. Oxford Methodism, a key element of Whitefield's early life, made him a disciplined man in his Bible reading, prayer, and penetrating introspection. Pietism gave Whitefield boldness with its rigorous devotional writings, most notably with *True Christianity* by Johann Arndt (1555–1621). The puritan-nonconformist tradition helped Whitefield to settle his theological convictions on topics like election, predestination, and the like. Finally, his own personal experience of the presence of the Holy Spirit deepened his hunger for a more dynamic life. Henry Scougal (1650–1678) and his powerful work, *The Life of God in the Soul of Man*, fed Whitefield's understanding and approach to having an immediate encounter with the presence of God. Thus, it can be seen that through this breadth of exposure that Whitefield's influences were catholic.

In the second chapter, Hindmarsh used the framework of an eighteenth-century cultural debate to think about the evangelical movement. This debate was popularized by Anglo-Irish author Jonathon Swift (1667–1745) in two satirical works: *A Tale of a Tub* (1704) and *The Battel of the Books* (1704). Both discussed the debate between ancient and modern authors holding sway over the current culture. Hindmarsh reveals that evangelicalism was a modern movement because it embraced several modern elements. It valued the subjective experience of God for its participants, it was a movement focused on social issues like slavery, and it was portrayed as something new, especially in terms of the revivals. Though these things had historical precedence in the church, the movement at that time produced something new and hence "modern."

The third chapter picks up on the ancient-modern debate by declaring that though the movement was indeed new, it truly had ancient roots. Early evangelicalism valued the Bible and it was formed through several important books. Hindmarsh returned to Scougal's *The Life of God in the Soul of Man* and he discussed *The Imitation of Christ* by Thomas à Kempis (1380–1471). Hindmarsh provides a kind of reception history of both pieces by early evangelicals and shows the popularity of the two works, the catholicity of early evangelicals, and their discerning approaches to these publications. Early evangelicals had simply been participating in retrieval in order to bring about something new.

Hindmarsh details the rise of Newtonianism in chapter four, with emphasis on how it influenced Wesley and Edwards. For Wesley, this influence stemmed from an interest in natural philosophy and empiricism—an interest in the former of these two was shared by Edwards. Hindmarsh finishes the chapter by displaying how this same interest impacted Charles Wesley (1707–1788) as can be seen in his hymn, "Author of every work Divine." Hindmarsh continues exploring how the rise of Newtonianism influenced evangelical spirituality in the subsequent chapter as well. Seven different evangelicals provide his framework: John Russell (1745–1806), Isaac Milner (1750–1820), Phillis Wheatley (1753–1784), Moses Browne (1704–1787), James Hervey (1714–1759), Anne Steele (1717–1778), and Augustus Toplady (1740–1778). The discussion of Newtonian influence on these individuals touched on topics like the Calvinist-Arminian debate, hymns, poetry, mathematics, and art. Thus, Hindmarsh illustrates that natural philosophy in had an impact on moral philosophy.

Chapters six and seven deal with early evangelicalism's perspective on the law. Hindmarsh argued, "In a way, evangelical spirituality was as much about the law as it was about anything else" (p.181). He establishes this through an assessment of evangelical preaching about the law, first of Whitefield, then through the preaching and popularity of lawyer and preacher Martin Madan (1725–1790). Next, he shows the evangelical use of the law through assize sermons, which were given on the occasion of the installation of a judge. Chapter seven continues this theme with a focus on the evangelical use of the law, but here Hindmarsh focuses on the devotional aspects of how the law fit into evangelical spirituality as well as how the law influenced evangelical soteriology.

Chapter eight finishes Hindmarsh's study of the relationship between evangelicalism and the broader eighteenth-century culture by looking more closely at art. The Calvinist-Arminian debate among early evangelicals, famously between Wesley and

Whitefield, even manifested itself in the art world. Simultaneously, two well-known artists of the day, Joshua Reynolds (1723–1792) and Thomas Gainsborough (1727–1788), had their own spat regarding style. Hindmarsh outlines some of the elements of their disagreement and discussed how various schools of art were forming at the time—schools that could be at loggerheads with one another at times. Hindmarsh likens this to the Calvinist-Arminian split within evangelicalism. He framed both of these theological approaches as schools of their own within evangelicalism, which had their own respective approaches to theology and spirituality. Hindmarsh argues that the Calvinist's goal in his or her spirituality was a contemplative sublime resting in the sovereignty of God. Yet, the Arminian's goal was more agonistic wanting to avoid any semblance of quietism.

In this work, Hindmarsh offers a fresh perspective on a familiar subject. While early evangelicalism is an oft-studied era, Hindmarsh's approach blends theology, spirituality, and culture. Frankly, this mixture is necessary to fully understand early evangelicalism in its context. Such an approach protects contemporary readers from seeing things that were not there in the early evangelical movement. Hindmarsh adequately explains the likely unfamiliar realms of science, law, and art to his readers so that his overall purpose in the book (merging evangelical theology and spirituality with aspects of the culture) was successful. A careful reader will likely begin to wonder how current cultural shifts in similar categories are impacting evangelicalism today.

Nicholas Abraham
The Southern Baptist Theological Seminary,
Louisville, KY

Andrew Fuller, *The Backslider: An Enquiry into the Nature, Symptoms, and Effects of Religious Declension, with the Means of Recovery* (1801, Minneapolis, MN: Curiosmith, 2016), 68 pages.

The Backslider by Andrew Fuller was originally published in 1801. A number of authors in the eighteenth century had written works with a similar title. For instance, the Scottish Presbyterian Ebenezer Erskine had one of his sermons published with the title of *The Backslider characterized* (1726) and the famous Charles Wesley even penned a hymn entitled "The backslider" (*c.*1760). Fuller's work, though, has stood the test of time and well merits the description by John Ryland as "an invaluable piece of practical divinity." This beautifully-typeset edition has an 1840 introduction by John Angell James (1785–1859), who pastored a Congregationalist church in Birmingham, England, for many years, and did not hesitate to describe the author of this tract as "one of the greatest theologians" of his day (p.7).

In 1801, when Fuller wrote this tract, England was locked in what amounted to a world war with France. Napoleon Bonaparte (1769–1821) was seeking to bring all of Europe under French domination. In 1801, England was all but alone in standing against the tyrant. Not surprisingly politics and the stratagems of war dominated the hearts and minds of many, including professing Christians. Fuller was not slow to recognize the way in which these concerns were infringing upon the sovereign claims of King Jesus. He thus spent some time discussing the way in which spiritual backsliding can be occasioned by too close an involvement in politics (p.24–29). Fuller was not a political quietist but he could see from the lives of some in his day that immersion in politics could be a major hindrance to the work of the Gospel. As he once told John Fountain (1767–1800), a missionary to India, "All political concerns are only affairs of this life with which he that will please him, who hath chosen him to be a soldier, must not entangle himself." There was much wisdom in these words for Fuller's day—and, it goes without saying, also for ours.

Michael A.G. Haykin
The Southern Baptist Theological Seminary
Louisville, KY

CENTER *for* BAPTIST STUDIES
at THE SOUTHERN BAPTIST THEOLOGICAL SEMINARY

The Andrew Fuller Center for Baptist Studies, located at The Southern Baptist Theological Seminary in Louisville, Kentucky, seeks to promote the study of Baptist history as well as theological reflection on the contemporary significance of that history. The center is named in honor of Andrew Fuller (1754–1815), the late eighteenth- and early nineteenth- century English Baptist pastor and theologian, who played a key role in opposing aberrant thought in his day as well as being instrumental in the founding and early years of the Baptist Missionary Society. Fuller was a close friend and theological mentor of William Carey, one of the pioneers of that society.

The Andrew Fuller Center holds an annual two-day conference in September that examines various aspects of Baptist history and thought. It also supports the publication of the critical edition of the Works of Andrew Fuller, and from time to time, other works in Baptist history. The Center seeks to play a role in the mentoring of junior scholars interested in studying Baptist history.

andrewfullercenter.org

DE GRUYTER

The Andrew Fuller Works Project
It is with deep gratitude to God that The Andrew Fuller Center for Baptist Studies announces that the publishing house of Walter de Gruyter, with head offices in Berlin and Boston, has committed itself to the publication of a modern critical edition of the entire corpus of Andrew Fuller's published and unpublished works. Walter de Gruyter has been synonymous with high-quality, landmark publications in both the humanities and sciences for more than 260 years. The preparation of a critical edition of Fuller's works, part of the work of the Andrew Fuller Center, was first envisioned in 2004. It is expected that this edition this edition will comprise seventeen volumes.

The importance of the project
The controlling objective of The Works of Andrew Fuller Project is to preserve and accurately transmit the text of Fuller's writings. The editors are committed to the finest scholarly standards for textual transcription, editing, and annotation. Transmitting these texts is a vital task since Fuller's writings, not only for their volume, extent, and scope, but for their enduring importance, are major documents in both the Baptist story and the larger history of British Dissent.

From a merely human perspective, if Fuller's theological works had not been written, William Carey would not have gone to India. Fuller's theology was the mainspring behind the formation and early development of the Baptist Missionary Society, the first foreign missionary society created by the Evangelical Revival of the last half of the eighteenth century and the missionary society under whose auspices Carey went to India. Very soon, other missionary societies were established, and a new era in missions had begun as the Christian faith was increasingly spread outside of the West, to the regions of Africa and Asia. Carey was most visible at the fountainhead of this movement. Fuller, though not so visible, was utterly vital to its genesis.

andrewfullercenter.org/the-andrew-fuller-works-project

H&E Publishing is a Canadian evangelical publishing company located out of Peterborough, Ontario. We exist to provide Christ-exalting, Gospel-centred, and Bible-saturated content aimed to show God to be as glorious and worthy as He truly is.

hesedandemet.com

www.ingramcontent.com/pod-product-compliance
Lightning Source LLC
Chambersburg PA
CBHW021118080526
44587CB00010B/558